BAITFISHING

Secrets of Baitfishing

by D.W. Bennett

ISBN 0-88839-087-4

Copyright © 1982 D.W. Bennett

Cataloging in Publication Data.

Bennett, D.W.
 Secrets of baitfishing
 (Northeast fishing series)

 1. Baitfishing. I. Title. II. Series.
 SH455.4.B45   799.1'2   C81-091032-2

All rights reserved. No part of this publication may be reproduced, stored in a retrieval system or transmitted, in any form or by any means, electronic, mechanical, photocopying, recording or otherwise, without the prior written permission of Hancock House Publishers.

Editor Margaret Campbell
Typeset by Anne Whatcott in Garamond type on an AM Varityper Comp/Edit
Layout Linda Rourke
Production & Cover Design Peter Burakoff
Artwork by Barb Wood
Printed by Friesen Printers, Altona, Manitoba, Canada
Front Cover Photo: David Hancock
Back Cover Photos (Top Right): Al Ristori
            (Top Left): Al Ristori
            (Bottom): Dery W. Bennett

Hancock House Publishers
256 Route 81, Killingworth, CT, U.S.A. 06417
Hancock House Publishers Ltd.
19313 Zero Avenue, Surrey, B.C., Canada V3S 5J9

Secrets of Baitfishing

Table of Contents

   Secrets of Baitfishing 6
1. Shellfish 9
2. Crabs 25
3. Worms 38
4. Shrimp 42
5. Fish 44
6. Chumming 62

Acknowledgments and Dedications

Among the many people I have talked to about marine life, marsh creatures, fish, and bait are: Jack Rudloe from Panacea, Florida, who owns Gulf Specimen Company; Joe LoPresti who runs Steven's Bait and Tackle in Long Branch, New Jersey, and talks bait and shares netting secrets whenever I phone or drop by; and a big, bulky man who sold bait and ran the hand-powered swing bridge behind Avalon, New Jersey. His last name must have been Cherry because his place was called Cherry's Dock, and he had what was probably the most basic bait house you can imagine. He used to sell me his old stock for half price, and he patiently showed me how to peel shedders and slice squid. Boy, did that place stink!

Frank Steimle of the Sandy Hook Marine Lab first showed me that going out seining for an hour was a profitable expenditure of time, and he knelt there on the wet seine and told me what those different critters were and where they came from.

John Woodward from Pottstown, Pennsylvania, showed me clam digging tricks on Cape Cod.

This book is for everyone out there scuffling around looking for something in the mud, sand and water. Keep at it — in the search is joy.

Author's Note

"It's time to fish or cut bait," someone is supposed to have said. I operate on the premise that all aspects of fishing are fun — right from the time you decide to go fishing through rigging the tackle, deciding when and where to go, getting to the spot, best of all, the first cast.

I also enjoy getting my own bait, not so much because it saves money — often it does not, given the extra equipment you might need — or because it saves time, but because it is another part of the fishing experience. It gets you close to the water, close to the fish's environment.

So I say try to catch your own bait whenever you can, even if you have to spend an extra hour doing it. But, and this is important, if the times you can fish are precious few, or if you are a total stranger to the area and its fish, don't hesitate to stop at the nearest bait store to buy bait and ask what's biting. It's not a crime to buy bait; often it makes a great deal of sense. But it's more fun if you get your own.

So let's change the saying. Let's say, "It's time to find bait and go fishing!"

Secrets of Baitfishing

About Bait

Bait is animal matter that you put on a hook to catch a fish. Bait is often called "natural bait," meaning that it is a natural substance, and that it usually occurs naturally. In other words, it is an animal that fish are likely to find while looking for something to eat. But what fish would be attracted to a chunk of clam that may have come from miles away and doesn't occur naturally in the fish's environment? The answer, in part, is that many fish feed by smell (taste), and that they are attracted to a chunk of bait whether it is a normal part of their diet, or merely something close to it.

The second kind of bait used for fishing is artificial, usually called lures, and includes such things as metal spoons, spinners, plugs, rubber eels, or feathers. These lures are designed to look like bait — like a fish — and they are fished with motion. Fish caught on lures are striking at the motion, or sometimes the sound, which could be the case if the lure is a surface popper.

The one major difference, then, is that natural bait appeals to the fish's senses of smell and sight, while artificial lures appeal to the fish's senses of sight and sound.

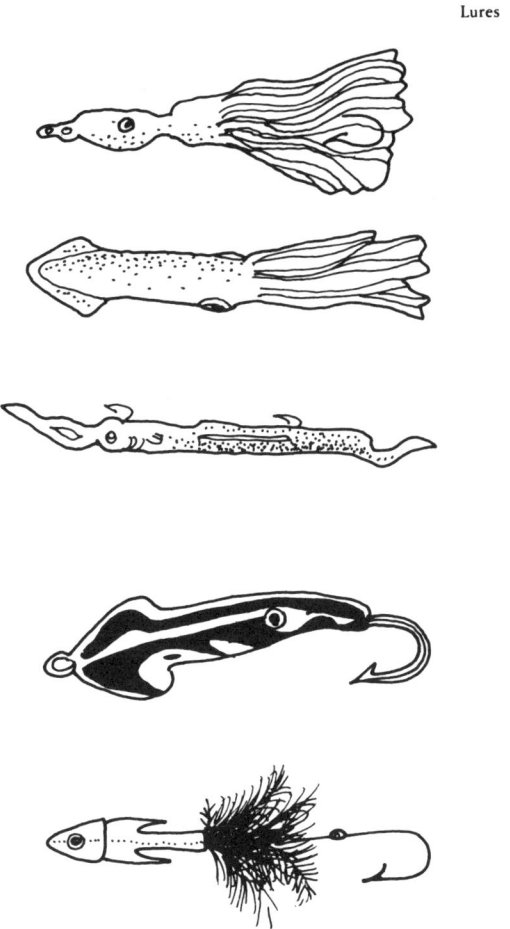

Lures

On the following pages, I have tried to catalog all the natural saltwater bait I know of that you can find by yourself by digging, netting, trapping, or catching with other bait. Mentioned along with the bait are some suggestions about what fish take what bait, but these are only general guides. At one time or another, most species of fish will eat almost anything they find in the sea. For example, a goosefish, which is not a usual game fish, has been found with seabirds in its stomach. Codfish eat sand dollars, and I have found bluefish that have eaten small puffers (blowfish). However, I do not recommend birds, sand dollars, or blowfish for bait.

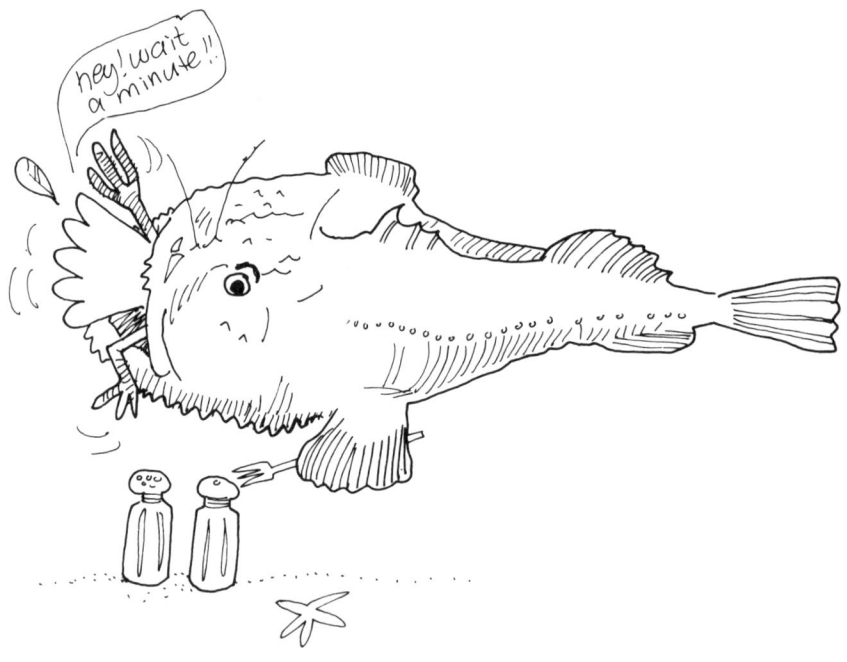

One final note: good bait is fresh bait, so keep what you get alive or cool, even frozen, but don't take more than you can use, and don't let bait go bad.

1. SHELLFISH

Clams, Mussels, Oysters.

I define shellfish as mollusks, bivalves — clams and such. Crabs, often considered shellfish, are covered separately.

Clams

In every season, clams are about the best bait. They are easy to find, they keep well, they are easy to use, and they catch fish. I used clam to catch my first big striped bass — a twenty-five pounder. The largest fish I have ever caught in the surf, a black drum, also bit a clam bait. About the only fish on the northeast coast that won't take a clam bait is the bluefish which, as a predator, really prefers moving live bait, shiny lures, or cut fish.

Surf Clams

Surf clams are ocean creatures found on the east coast from Long Island to Cape Hatteras. They live anywhere from the surf line on out to depths of about eighty feet. Also called skimmer clams, they grow as large as seven inches across, and are the largest of the clams found on this coast. They live buried in the sand, sharp side down. In the summer, when the water is warm, moss grows on the top of the shell. When you see a surf clam in shallow water, it looks like a small, oblong growth of moss.

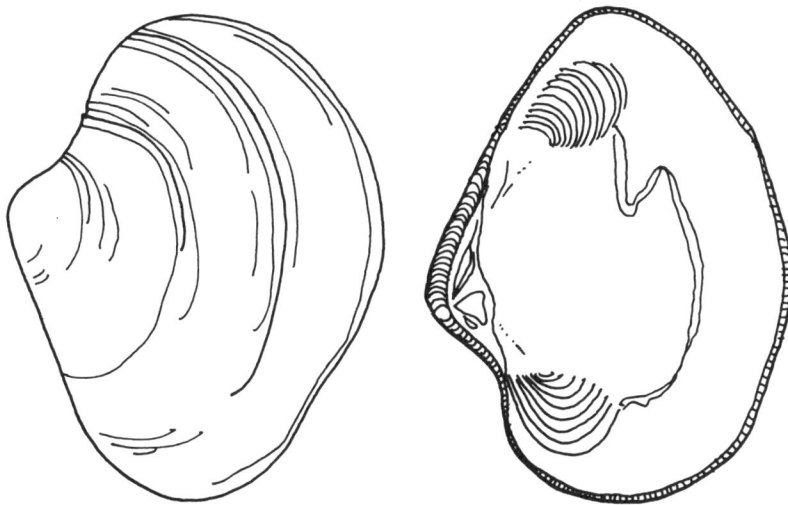

There are a number of places to find surf clams. After a storm, they are often found right at the tide line, tossed up out of their beds and onto dry land. Pick up only the live ones. You can test them by giving them a gentle squeeze. If the clam tries to close its shell, it is alive. Clams can also be found on the first sand bar that forms offshore. The best time to look is during a dead low tide. Wade or swim out onto the bar and look for the patch of moss, or for a keyhole-shaped hole, perhaps with watermarks around it where the clam has squirted. It is possible to find surf clams on a bar that is covered with water. Again, you must look for the mossy patches. You can find them by digging blindly on the bar, but in this case you are trusting to luck.

Surf clams will keep for a few days in a cool shaded place, especially in a wet burlap bag, and they'll keep for about a week when iced. But don't let them drown, either in salt or fresh water. And they freeze well; that is, freezing doesn't soften clam meat as much as it does with other bait.

To open or shuck a surf clam, insert a knife between the shells and cut the two adductor muscles; there is one at each end of the shell. The meat can then be scooped out and cut into chunks or strips. The thin meat along each lip is also good for bait, but the adductor muscles won't stay on a hook.

Adductor muscles

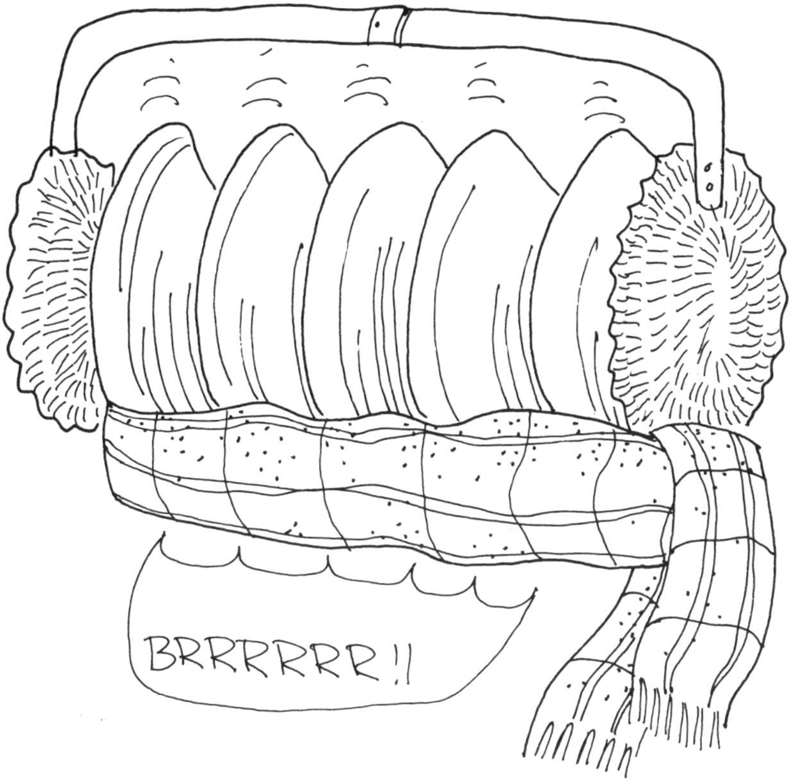

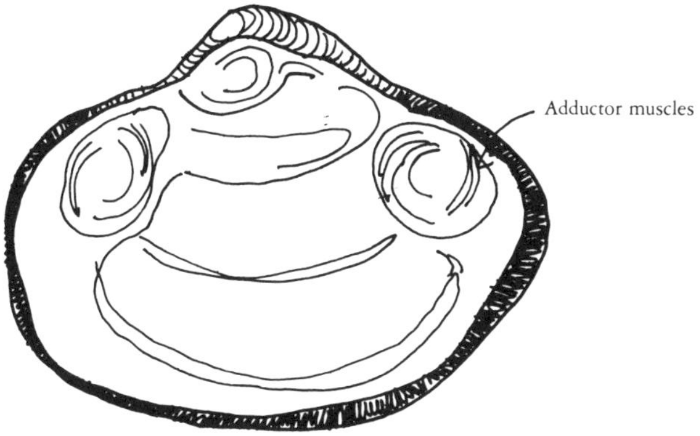

You can get about five or six pieces of bait from a surf clam when fishing for black seabass, porgy, and the like. For striped bass and other big fish, use the whole thing. In fact, let the size of your hook determine the size of the bait.

By the way, surf clams, in fact any clams, are also very good bait for crabs.

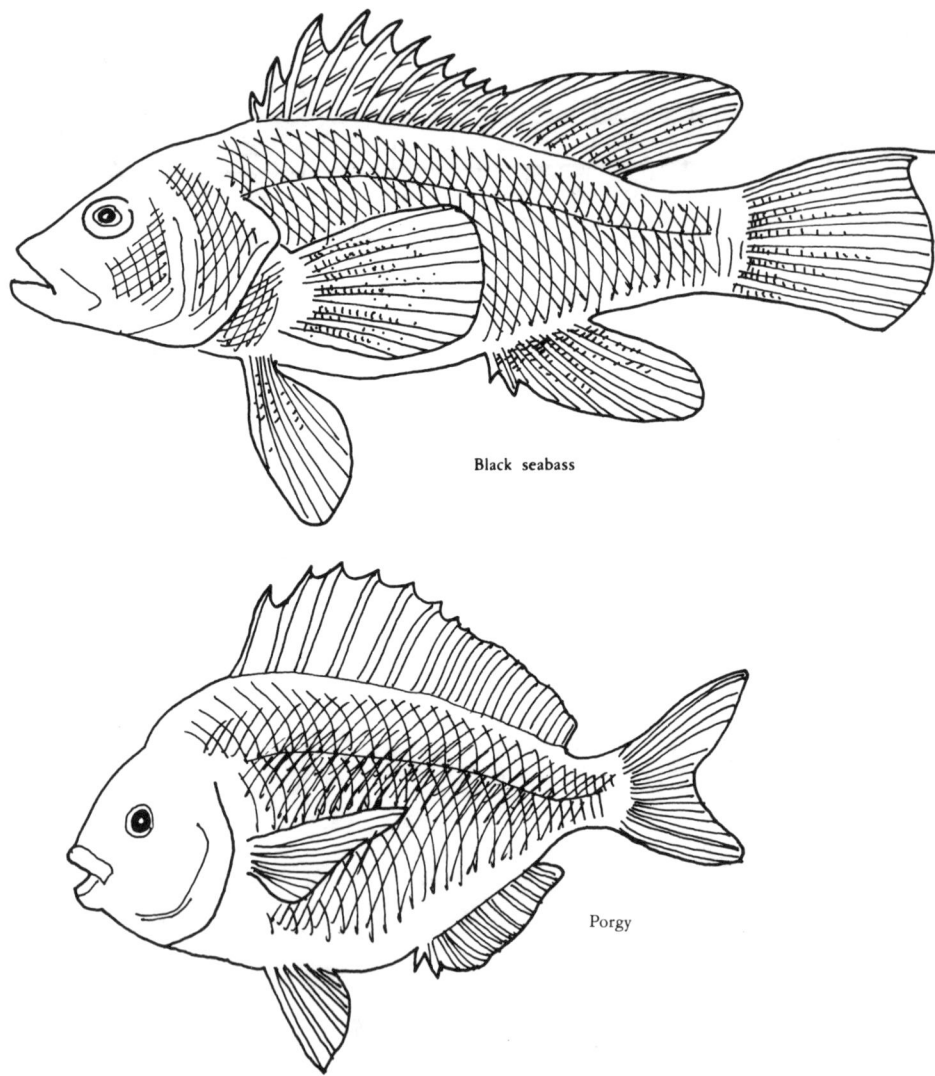

Black seabass

Porgy

Hard Clams

Hard clams differ from surf clams in a number of ways. They live in bays, tidal rivers, and estuaries, rather than in the open

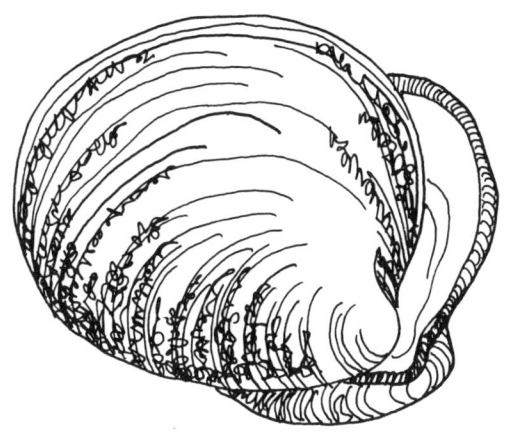

CLAMP

ocean. They are usually found in mud or muddy sand, but rarely in sand alone. They do not show themselves at or near the surface unless you run across one that has been washed out of its bed and is trying to dig back in. And while surf clams, even when closed as tightly as possible, still have a gap between the shells, hard clams can really "clam up."

Hard clams are also called quahogs (ko hogs) in the areas north of eastern Long Island. They are the raw clams served at restaurants and clam bars under the names little necks and cherry stones. Big hard clams, five inches or more across, are called chowders.

You can find these clams by finding a likely spot and stomping around in the mud, feeling for clams with your feet. Or, if you don't like getting your feet dirty, you can rake them. Also, at very low tides, you can find clams in mud or sand bars, often with a small squirt hole showing their location.

Be warned that states have shellfish laws governing the taking of hard clams, and the soft and razor clams which are discussed later. These laws cover how many you can dig and where you can dig. Many productive hard clam beds are closed to shellfishing because of pollution. This is to prevent these clams from entering the raw clam market. Clams feed by drinking in water and straining out food. If the water is full of pollutants and bacteria, the clams will be too. Don't think that as long as you are only digging for bait you can dig for polluted clams. The wardens have heard that one; it doesn't work. So check local laws before you dig.

Hard clams are hard to open, but that's not how they got their name. They're called hard clams because their shell is thick and tough. You can shuck hard clams like surf clams — by inserting a knife between the shells and slicing the adductor muscles. But don't try this method unless you know how to do it. Beginners usually end up with unopened clams and hands opened with cuts.

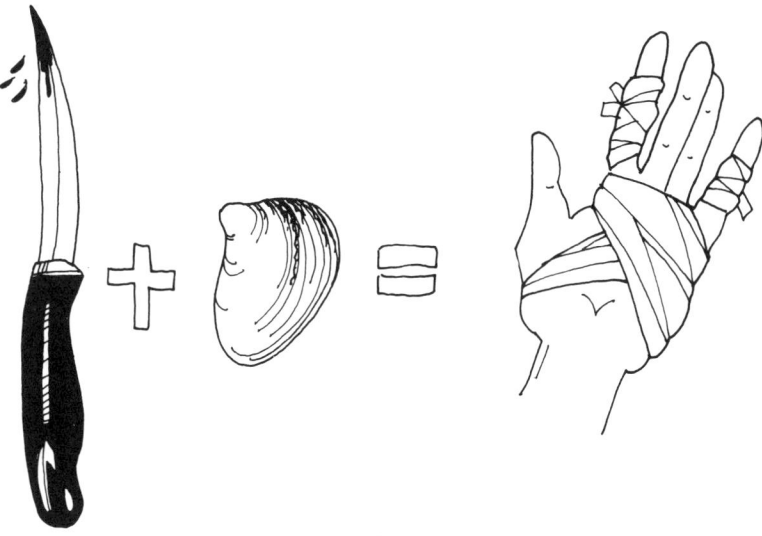

The easiest way to shuck hard clams is to bang the clam against a hard object — a rock or another clam — then reach in with a knife, cut the muscles, and scoop out the meat. Again, from one clam you can make one to eight baits, depending upon the size of your hook.

I use hard clams for bait only as a last resort. If the clam bed is open for shellfishing, and you have a licence, it makes better sense to dig a mess of clams and then take **them** home for dinner. But, if you really need bait and you really want to fish, hard clams are good.

Soft Clams and Razor Clams

Soft clams and razor clams are found in the same general areas as the hard clams, though usually in places with a more sandy bottom. At low tide, soft clams show themselves with siphon holes and little water marks where they have squirted.

If you walk along a soft clam bar at low tide, you will see the clams squirt just a step ahead and to each side of you. Then you will see why one of their nick-names is "piss clams."

They're also called steamers. These are the clams that are served steamed, are dipped in broth and melted butter, and are then popped down the hatch.

Soft clams are exactly that — very soft. Their shell is delicate, and you will probably break the shells of half of those you dig until you learn the knack of digging next to the hole not right on top of it.

Soft clams have soft bodies — almost as soft as an oyster — so they don't stay on the hook well. I take along a spool of thread when I am using soft clams, and gently wrap the bait after hooking it.

Soft clam harvesting is also governed by state laws. Watch for closed areas, limits on numbers, size restrictions, and days when clam digging is illegal. Check these laws **before** you dig.

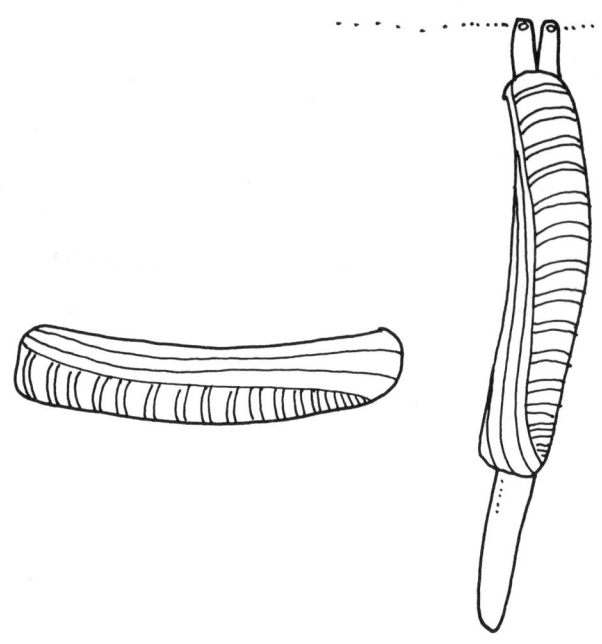

Razor clams are found in the same beds as soft clams, but you are likely to find 100 soft clams for every razor clam. They are shaped like an old safety razor, and they can dig down with lightning speed so they are hard to catch. They are really a bait of last resort. Use them like soft clams. They're very good for bottom fish, and especially good for winter flounder.

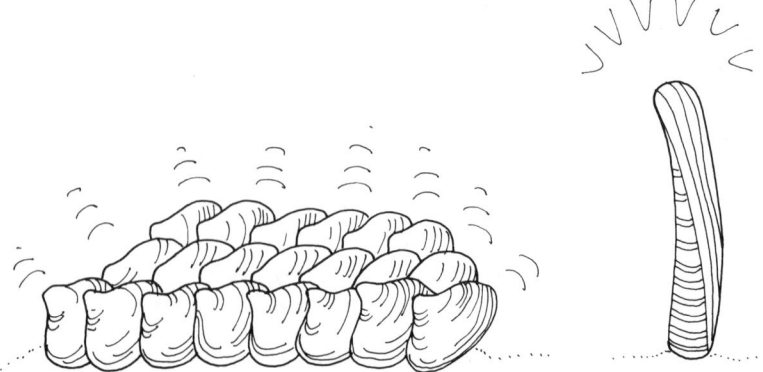

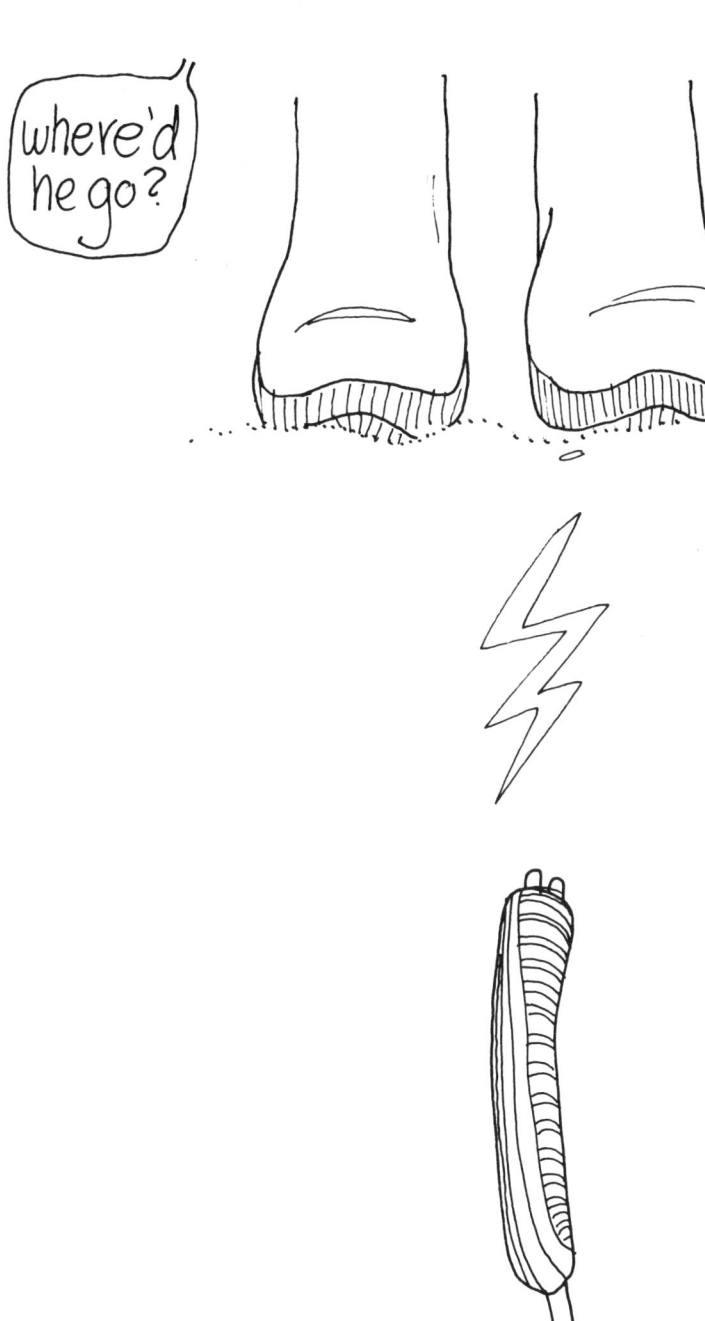

Oysters

Oysters are listed here only because there have been a few times when I was baitless on a shore in the Chesapeake and had an hour to kill. I dug three or four oysters, baited a small hook, and had a lot of fun with some small spot or lafayette (also called Cape May Goodies.) However, it's really a shame to waste an oyster by using it as bait.

Again, oysters are covered by strict laws. So in general, leave them alone, unless you are stuck on a desert island.

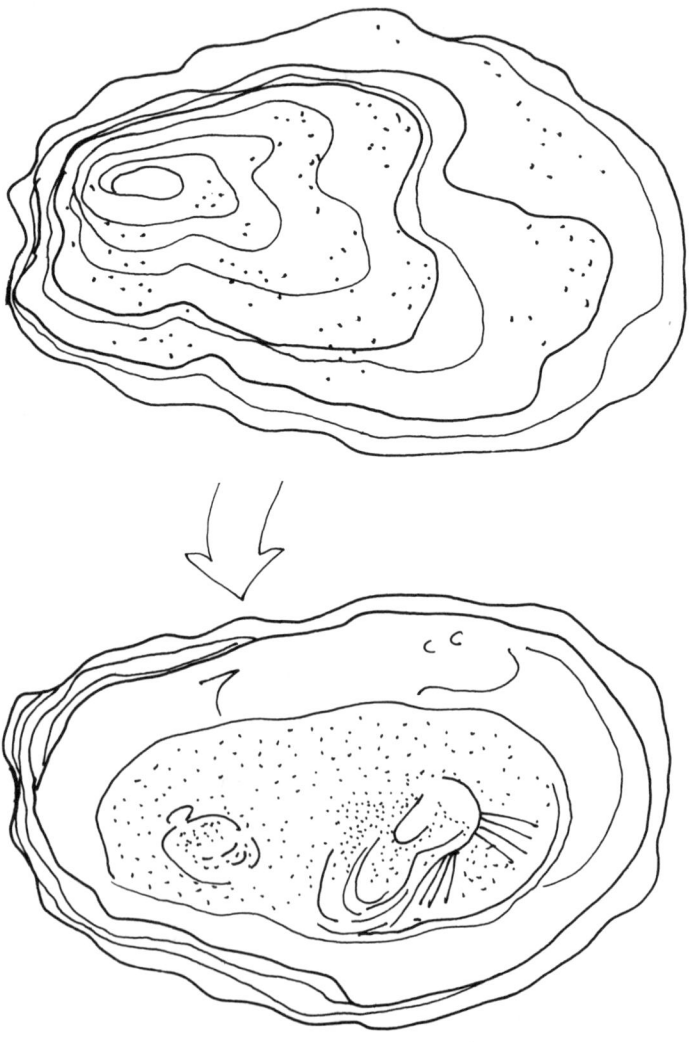

Mussels

Mussels are dark-colored bivalves that live attached to rocks or dug into marshes. There are three mussels common to the northeast coast: horse mussels and blue mussels, which are ocean dwellers and not good for bait, and ribbed mussels. Ribbed mussels are marsh dwellers and are good bait.

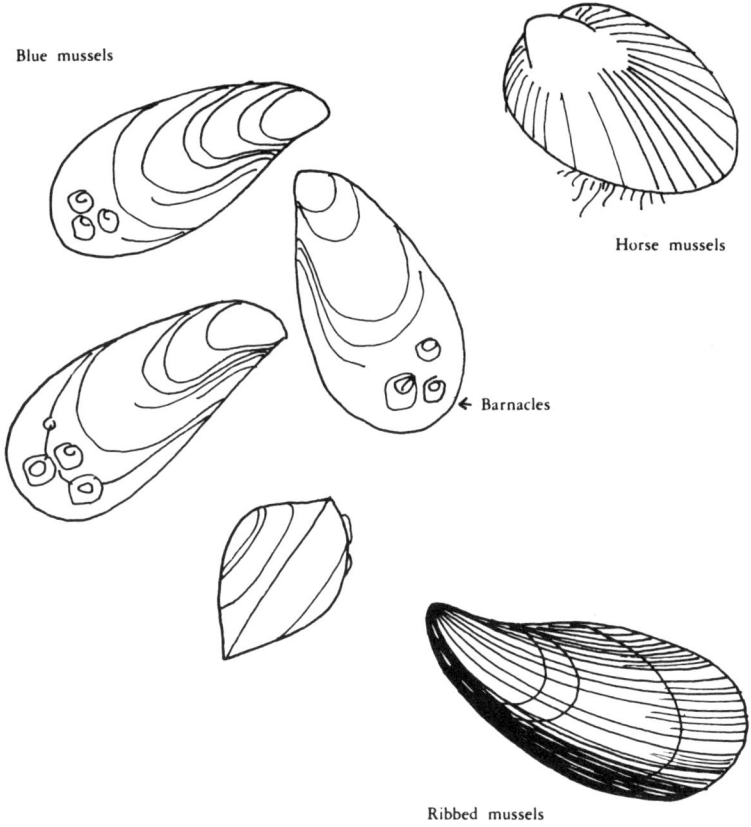

Blue mussels

Horse mussels

← Barnacles

Ribbed mussels

Ribbed mussels are so named because they have ribbed or ridged shells. Horse mussels and blue mussels are smooth. You can find ribbed mussels at the high tide line in salt marshes and along salt tidal creeks. They bury themselves in the mud with the hinge down, so what you will see showing are the tips of the two shells. Work your fingers down along the mussel an inch or so, get a firm grip, and twist the mussel. This breaks the threads (byssus) that the mussel uses to anchor itself. Now you can pull the mussel out. I collect only good-sized ones — at least three inches long.

Mussels are too soft to hold on a hook unless they have been prepared. To prepare a mussel, put half an inch of water in a pot and bring to a roaring boil. Add the mussels and cover tightly. Steam them for about thirty seconds, or until the shells just begin to gape. This is to get the mussels open, not to cook them. As soon as the shells begin to open, flood them with cold water. Shuck the mussel into a jar by cutting the adductor muscle and scooping out the meat.

After shucking add regular table salt to the jar — about one tablespoon per six meats. Stir and add just enough water to cover, then let the mussels sit overnight. The salt toughens and preserves the meat. You can use them twelve hours after preparation, and they will keep unrefrigerated.

Even when treated in this way, the mussels are still somewhat soft, so you must tie them on the hook with fine thread. Just impale the mussel on the hook as best you can, and then take about ten to fifteen loose turns with some thread. Mussels are super bait for bottom fish.

All mussels are good for chumming. They can be used fresh. Just crunch them lightly with a mallet or board and pour them into your chum pot (see chumming later).

Other shellfish can be used for bait: whelks, limpets, and moonsnails, for example. But many of these are very tough and, while they stay on the hook well, some may be so tough that the fish can bite without getting through the meat to the hook. So if you use them, use strips of flesh and leave the barb of the hook showing.

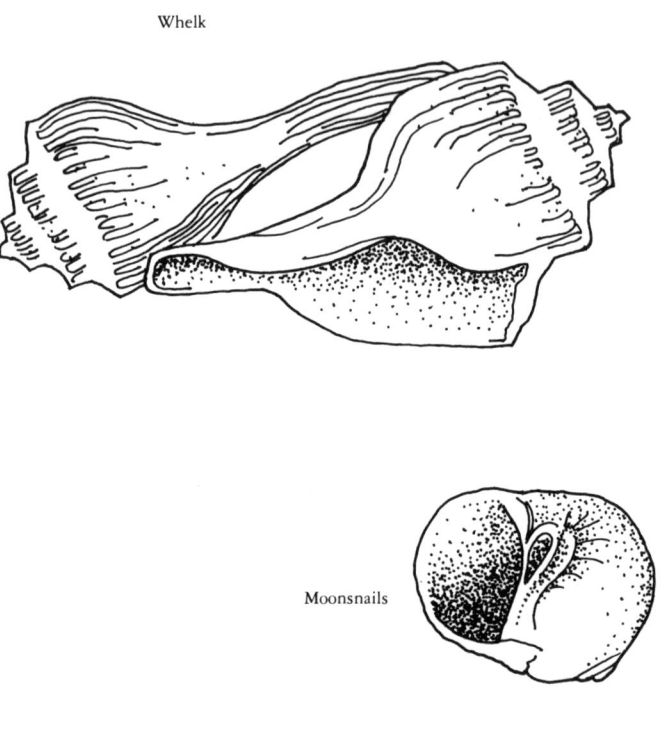

Whelk

Moonsnails

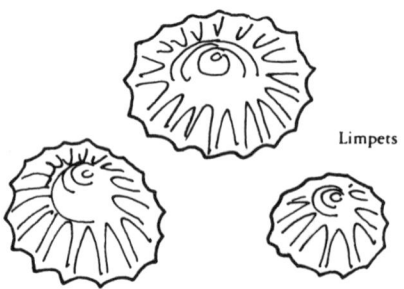

Limpets

2. CRABS

Crabs form a major part of the diet of most bottom-feeding fish. Biologists have found codfish chock full of large, offshore, deepwater crabs. Weakfish have a special fondness for small blue crabs, and striped bass at times feed in the surf on soft calico crabs to the exclusion of all other food. So crabs are superior bait.

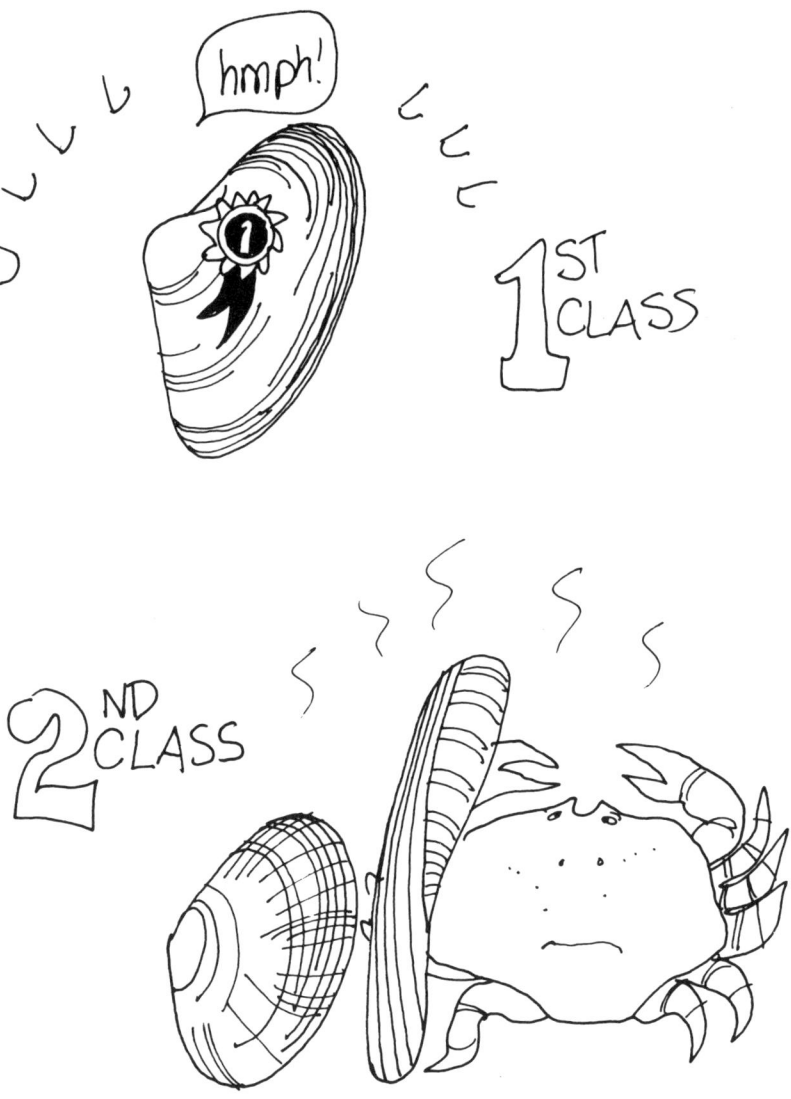

The problem is that when they are hard-shelled, they are difficult to fish. The hook, deeply imbedded in a hard crab, will not penetrate the crab shell when a fish bites, and most crabs are too big to be fished whole. So the answer is to use them when they are soft, or, when they are hard, to learn how to prepare them as bait.

All crabs have hard external skeletons. To grow, they must shed their shells periodically. They do this often when they are young and growing quickly, and less often when they are mature. The trick is to find crabs when they are soft — when they are called softshells or softies — so let's cover that part first. Then I'll share some ideas about using hard crabs.

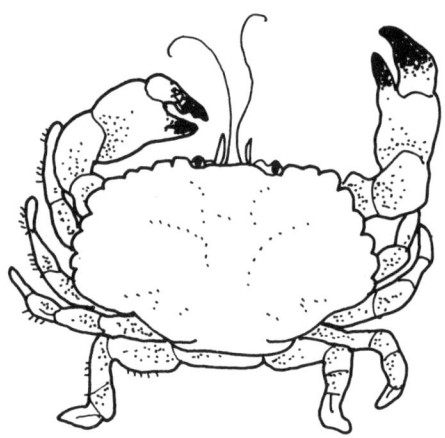

Blue Crabs

Blue crabs are creatures of estuaries, marshes, and tidal rivers. Soft blue crabs are one of the best baits around, but soft crabs are also superior table fare. So if you catch some, you should consider frying them up for dinner rather than using them for bait. But if it's bait you're after, blue crab softies are fine.

Crabs cannot feed right after they shed. Until their new shell hardens (about twenty-four hours), they remain hidden. The best way to catch them is by pulling a seine through the shallows, or by wading the shallows with a scoop net and looking for them under things.

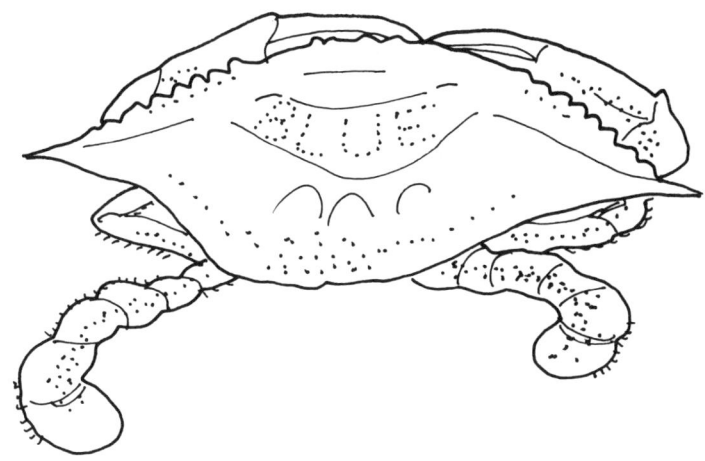

A soft crab is just that, totally soft. As bait, you can cut them to any size you wish. I find that each claw of a good-sized crab will make two baits, and that the body will make another four to eight. Soft crabs will keep for days in damp seaweed in a refrigerator, and they can be frozen.

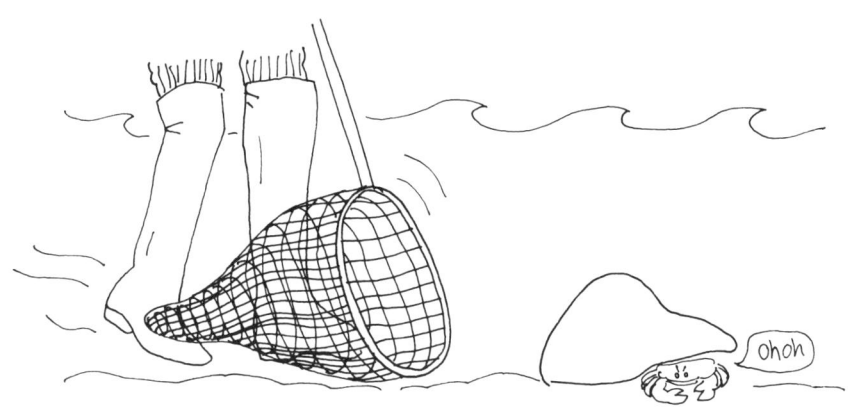

Shedders are crabs that are almost ready to shed their shells. They are also called busters. A new shell has grown underneath their old shell and the old shell is preparing to split. You can tell them from regular hard crabs by their slower movements, but the *best* way to tell a shedder is to feel the shell on the under side of the body where the shell comes to its points. If the crab is a shedder, the shell there will be soft, and you can see it beginning to separate. A word of warning here: handle blue crabs carefully, they are pugnacious and well-armed!

Small shedders can be fished whole or cut in half. Larger shedders can provide up to seventeen baits for smaller bottom-feeding fish.

To prepare a shedder for bait, cut or break off the claws and legs. Then tear the shell off the top of the crab by peeling the apron (the flap on the bottom of the crab). When you tear off the hard shell, you will see a duplicate soft shell underneath. Peel this soft shell off and cut it in half. You have your first two pieces of bait. Then cut the crab in half, right and left, and then cut crosswise, so that each piece includes one joint, remaining from either a leg or a claw. This produces ten baits. The soft under-apron is bait number thirteen, and each claw, carefully deshelled, provides another two.

Hard blue crabs can be used somewhat like shedders, but they need more preparation. Start by breaking off the claws and legs. The claw meat cannot be used for bait; I save the claws and boil them up for a meal or snack.

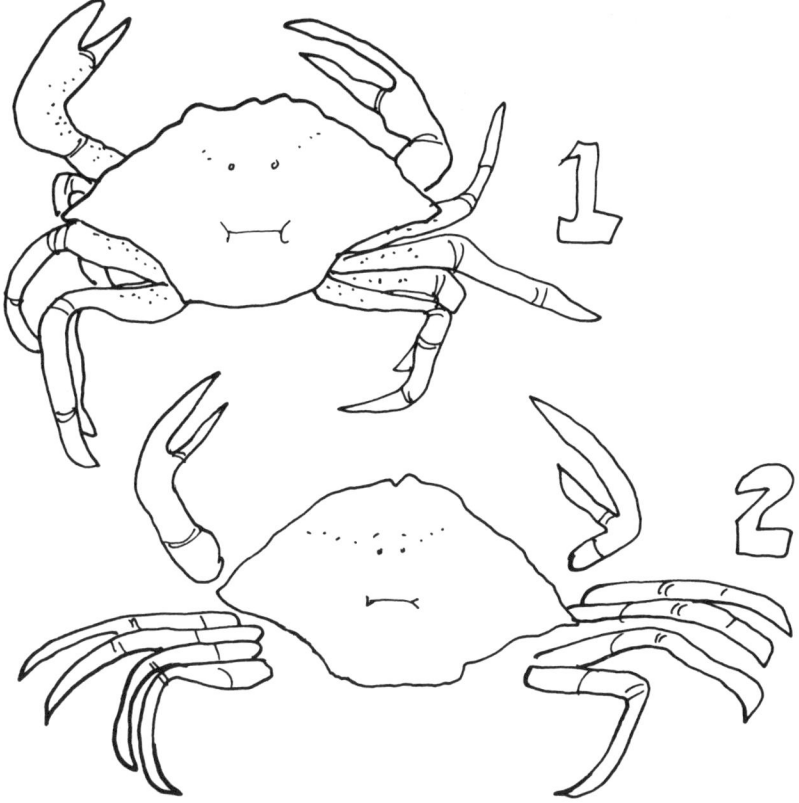

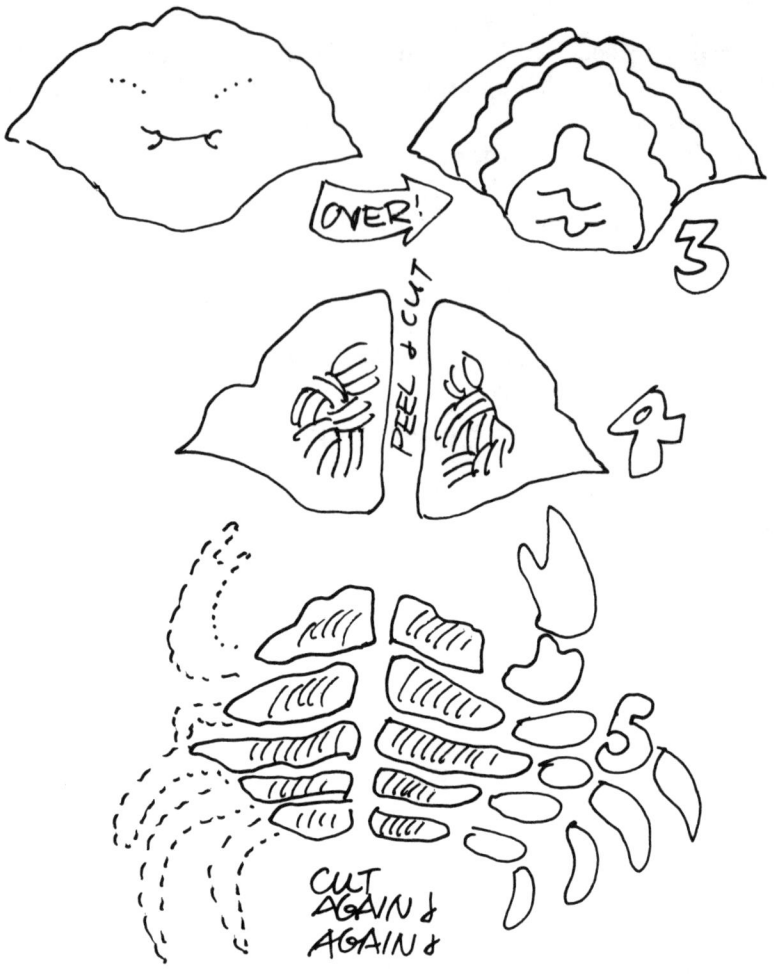

Tear off the top shell and cut the crab in half and then across, leaving a joint with each piece, the same as with a shedder. But with hard crabs, you must cut or pull away as much of the hard shell as you can so that the meat is exposed, especially from the bottom shell. Then hook the resulting pieces so that the hook's barb is not buried in or shielded by hard shell; otherwise the fish will bite but cannot be hooked.

While the blue crabs live in bays and are seldom found in the ocean, they make good bait in the surf and sometimes even offshore. I recall a cod fisherman who swore by blue crabs when others used clam bait. He said crabs caught bigger cod.

Calico Crabs

Calico crabs live in the ocean's shallow water, usually right in the surf. They are the crabs that nip at your feet when you are standing in shallow water. They are also called lady crabs. They are usually two to four inches across, and have pink, red, and brown patterned shells. Softshells and shedders are used almost exclusively, though big hard calicos can be prepared and used like blue crabs.

To catch soft calicos, you need a special rake which you can buy in hardware or bait stores, or which you can make yourself. It looks like a garden rake with about eight to twelve tines, each four inches long. Atop the rake is a small net or wire basket.

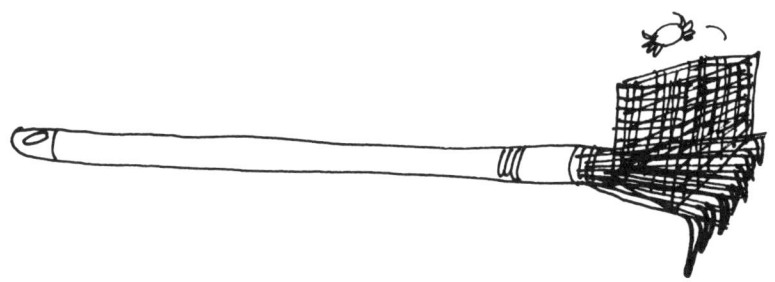

The best time to rake calicos is at low tide, and there seem to be more softies during periods of the full moon. Look for them in the sloughs between the beach proper and a sandbar, during June, July, and August. Calicos move offshore in cool weather. Often you will see lots of crab shells on the beach — these are shed shells and mark a good spot.

To rake, place the rake in the sand and its handle on your shoulder. Grasp the handle with both hands in front of you halfway between waist and chest level. Then walk backward, using the pressure of your hands to keep the rake's tines digging into the sand. As you drag, you will feel the rake striking things — shells and crabs. When you want to check to see what is in the rake's bag, pull the tines out of the sand and turn the rake over as you pull it out of the water.

I usually check the crabs I have caught, taking the softies first, and handling them very gently. I use a soft canvas bag to keep the crabs in. Then I check the other crabs. Shedders go in a different compartment of the bag and the hard calicos go back into the water.

After you have raked awhile, you will be able to feel the difference between the shells and crabs, but softies are hard to feel. I have often pulled up the rake thinking it was empty and have found a handful of softies.

On busy fishing beaches, you will come across some bonuses — riggings and lures. That makes crab raking a kind of outing in itself, a happy mixture of fishing and beachcombing.

Soft calicos are prime bait for striped bass during the summer months. Use a standard bottom rig. This is a weight on the end of your line with a hook on a leader attached to the line a few inches away from the weight. I use whole calicos unless they are very big, in which case I cut them in half. I tie soft calicos on with a short piece of thread.

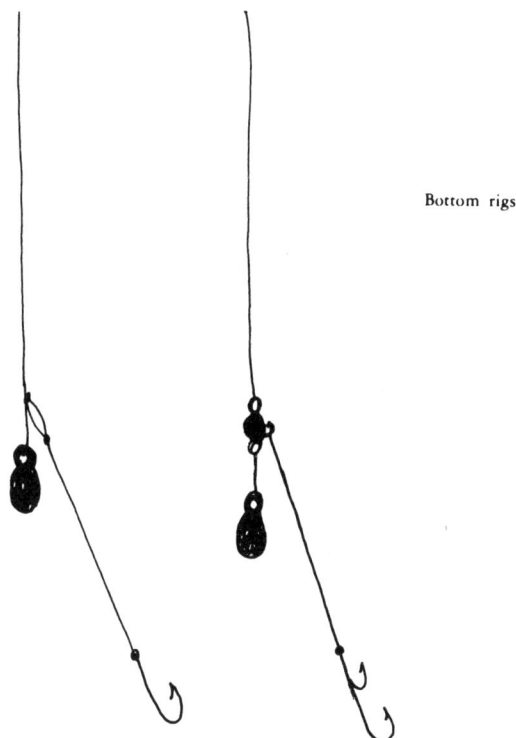

Bottom rigs

Mole Crabs

Mole crabs are the egg-shaped little fellows that dash up and down the summer beaches, riding the waves at the surf line. They are crustaceans, but not true crabs; instead they are a sort of cross between shrimp and crabs.

Mole crabs can be raked out of the surf at almost any tide. I usually pick a beach where there are plenty of hard mole crabs at a time when they are moving around, and simply dig or rake through the sand just a little offshore of the surf. The big mole crabs are almost always females and grow as large as an inch long. Males are seldom longer than half an inch.

Soft mole crabs are very good bait for surf-fishing for kingfish, striped bass, and weakfish. Hard moles can be used, but I have had very little luck with them. If you do use them, place the hook in them in such a way that the barb is not sheathed by the shell.

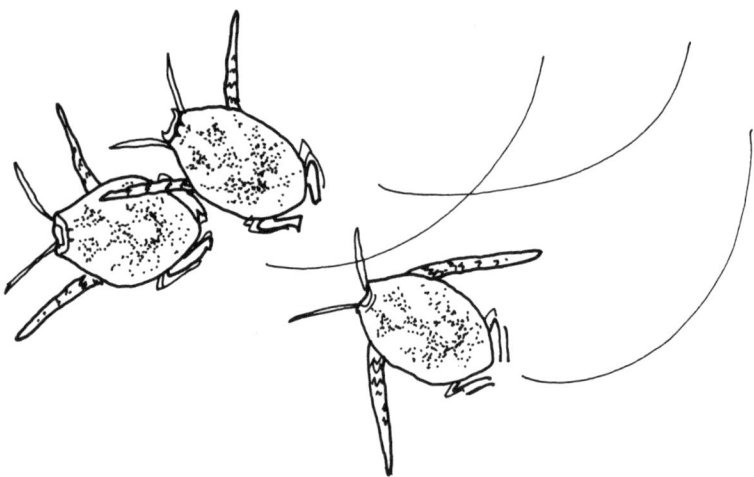

Fiddler Crabs

Fiddler crabs are especially good bait for tautog or blackfish, although interestingly, tautog seldom eat fiddlers as a normal part of their diet. Tautog feed almost exclusively on mussels, which they can tear off pilings or rocks with their strong teeth and then grind with other teeth called pharyngeals, located at the back of the mouth. But fiddlers are superb tautog bait.

Fiddler crabs live in salt marshes housed in burrows in, or near,

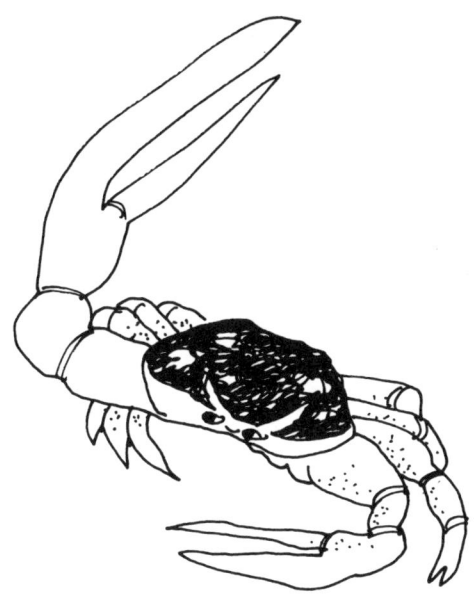

salt marsh grasses. They come out of their burrows as the tide drops and feed on matter washed up by the tide.

To catch fiddlers, locate a marsh where they are plentiful and get there as the tide drops. Wear your worst clothes and chase them down, catching them by hand or with a crab net with a straight top so you can drag it across the ground (see section on dip nets).

To prepare a fiddler crab for bait, break off the large claw if the crab has one (males do), and hook them through the back. It doesn't matter if you bury the barb.

Green Crabs

Green crabs grow as large as five inches across and look somewhat like a chunky blue crab, but without the points on the ends of the shell. Also, green crabs do not have the swimming flipper on the last leg. Green crabs are found in seaweed, under rocks, and in rock crevices. Look for them also in holes in seawalls and jetties. They do not move fast and can be picked up by hand.

They do not have the bad temper of blue and calico crabs. Small green crabs are good blackfish bait.

Hermit Crabs

Hermit crabs have the interesting habit of using the shells of other animals — usually snails and drills — for their homes. As hermit crabs feel that they are outgrowing their shells, they look for bigger ones. When they find a suitable one, they line up close to it, pull their soft bodies out of the old shells and pop into the new. It is that soft body of the hermit crab that is good bait for bottom fish. I have especially good luck fishing with hermit crab tails for kingfish (northern whiting).

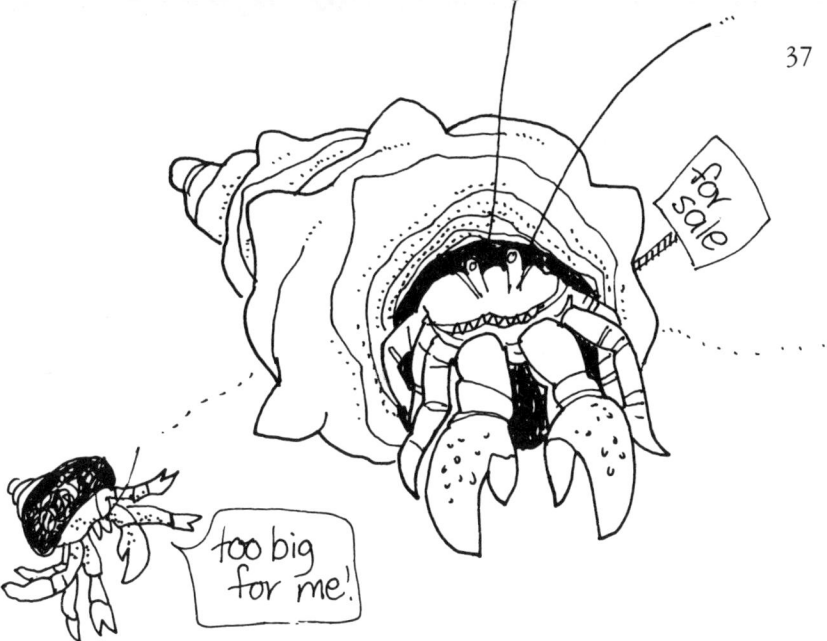

Hermit crabs are found at the mouths of tidal rivers and estuaries, usually near the tide line. To remove the crab from his home, crack open the shell and pull the animal out. Use only the soft tail.

Lobster Tails

Lobster tails are good bait. I have used them for striped bass, for fluke, and I have caught seabass and porgy on them, but that was when lobster was fifty cents a pound in south Jersey. Nowadays, a lobster large enough to have in your possession is large enough to eat. But they are good bait if you care to try.

3. WORMS

There are hundreds of species of marine worms which live from the upper, almost freshwater, tidal reaches of rivers out to the edge of the continental shelf. These worms range in size from microscopic up to the four- or five-foot long tapeworm. Worms are an important part of the marine food chain. They are eagerly sought after as food by fish and crabs, and worms, in turn, can feed as predators, browsers (on algae), or scavengers.

As with freshwater fishing, you find worms by digging. The problem is to find out where to dig. Here are some general tips; they apply to several species of worms that are common and big enough to be sought after for bait.

Dig marine worms at low tide in mud or muddy sand. You seldom find worms in the sticky kind of mud that can suck your shoes off. Look for relatively firm footing — ground that is not firm or hard, but that is not "squishy" either. Use a pitch fork or manure fork. Simply dig up the ground and turn it over, looking for worms in the clod you have removed, or around the edge of the hole you have just created.

The best places to try are on mud flats near sandy beaches, on the backside of barrier islands, near inlets, and up rivers where streams enter. Often you will find worms right in with soft clams at low tide. Also, try turning over pieces of driftwood that may be lodged in the mud.

If, after a few digs, you don't find anything, move about ten yards in any direction. Keep moving, digging trial holes. Sooner or later, as you dig in different places at different times, you will get a feel of when to dig and where the worms are. Then you can come back to that place.

Also, if I have located a spot where I can be assured of finding a bunch of worms in about an hour, I then cover up the places I have dug. By so doing I don't mar the area for further digging, or mark it for others who might be looking for worms on the next tide. I'm not saying be nasty, I'm just saying that you need not share your favorite worm spot with strangers.

There are several kinds of worms commonly used for bait along the northeast coast:

Blood Worms

Blood worms are smaller than nightcrawlers, blood red, delicate, and expensive. The major area where these are dug commercially is in Maine. It's backbreaking work. Bloodworms are unsurpassed as bait for winter flounder, small saltwater "panfish," spot, and kingfish. Also, anglers in the Massachusetts Bay area use them in the winter for smelt. Bloodworms have a set of pincers on their heads that can give you a painful nip, so handle with care.

Sand Worms

Sand worms, more common from Massachusetts south, are bigger (they grow up to ten inches long) and thicker than bloodworms. They are prime bait for striped bass and weakfish.

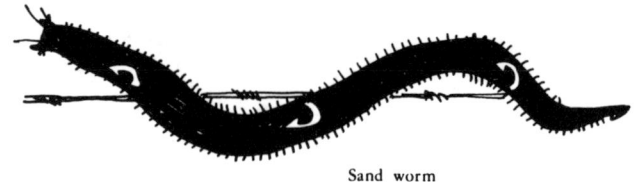

Sand worm

Ribbon or Tapeworms

Ribbon or tapeworms are giant (up to four feet long), very fragile worms that you may be lucky enough to find. They are good bait in pieces but very difficult to keep. When you find one, draw it gently from its hole or it will break.

Greenworms

Green worms are found on both ocean and bay beaches. They are green, about the size of a blood worm, and are very good bait.

Some general tips on worms:

-- If you break a worm in half, do not put those halves in with your whole worms. The halves die very quickly and they will kill the rest of your worms. Either throw those pieces away or, better yet, keep them separately and use them first (that day).

-- Worms can be kept for two to three days in damp seaweed in a refrigerator, but check them frequently. If one dies, they all die quickly.

-- With worms, follow the old adage: "Big bait — big fish." When fishing for stripers or weakfish, use a whole worm and keep it strung out so it looks like a worm. For winter flounder, use tiny pieces, maybe an inch or so in length.

-- You can use freshwater or garden worms (earthworms, nightcrawlers) for bait in salt water. They are not as good as marine worms, but I have caught plenty of flounders on small earthworms. If you use them, replace your bait often — they die and bleach out quickly.

4. SHRIMP

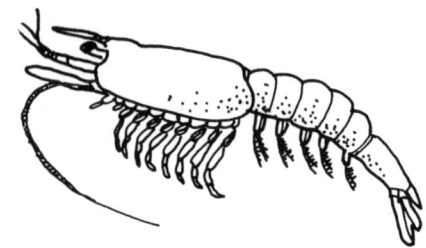

There are two kinds of inshore shrimp common along the northeast coast that are easy to catch and make good bait. There is the sand shrimp, more commonly found north of Cape Cod, and the mud (or grass or shore) shrimp, which is more common from Cape Cod south. Both shrimps are about two inches long, light colored, and almost transparent. Although they look very much alike, they are of different genera. They can be found from inlets into esuaries and back bays, and up tidal rivers to almost fresh water. Sand shrimp are also found sometimes along the ocean beach.

Shrimp are most easily caught with a fine-mesh net, one or two-person seines, or large-mouth dip nets. See the next section on fish for details on different types of nets.

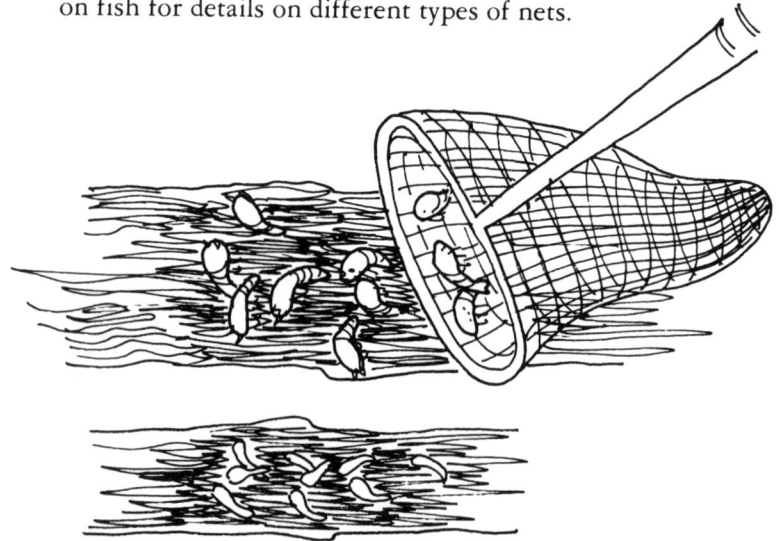

You will often catch shrimp when you are netting bait fish. The best places to look for them are in and around grassy bottoms, at the mouths of creeks, or around docks, pilings, and bulkheads.

Like other animals that move about, there will be times when the shrimp are thick and other times when they are very tough to find. Try different tides and times of day. Sooner or later, you will learn their patterns, and when it is best to go after them.

Most often, shrimp are right on the bottom or dug into the sand, so when you drag a net, be sure it hugs the bottom. Shrimp also like to cling to pilings. I have often caught a mess by walking along a dock and pulling a dip net against the pilings upward to the surface. You can also find them clinging to old bulkheads but avoid new ones with fresh preservative — they are not fruitful.

Shrimp can be kept in a livewell or minnow box, or they can be kept nested in damp seaweed. But don't try to keep them in a bucket of water unless the bucket has a top — shrimp will jump up onto the bucket's sides and then out. Also, like minnows, they do better in damp seaweed, or even damp newspaper, than they do in water. (See the next section.)

Shrimp are good bait for weakfish, striped bass, and for any small bottom fish, but because they are so small, it is sometimes necessary to thread two or three on a hook. They are also good chum to attract fish if you have enough. When fishing for weakfish, I can go through two quarts in a tide.

Here is how I fish with shrimp chum:

Find a likely place — I'll leave that up to you — to anchor your boat. Then start dribbling live shrimp over the side, three per minute to start with. Pinch some and kill them so they sink. Then bait with a few shrimp (or you can use some worms for bait). Often the string of shrimp drifting with the tide will attract weakfish and you can catch a bunch.

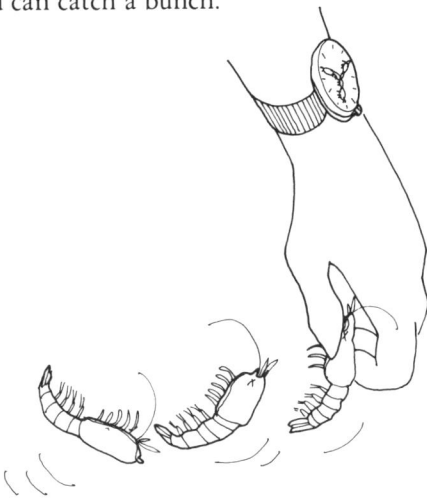

5. FISH

Fish are the all-round bait. They can be used effectively in a variety of different ways — live or dead, whole or in pieces, or fresh, salted or frozen. You can use a piece from a game fish as bait and you can have baitfish for dinner.

Before we cover how to catch certain special fish for bait, however, we should go into some detail about the equipment you may want to have on hand to catch them.

Using nets is probably the easiest, fastest way to catch baitfish. Nets can be used best in water up to three or four feet deep.

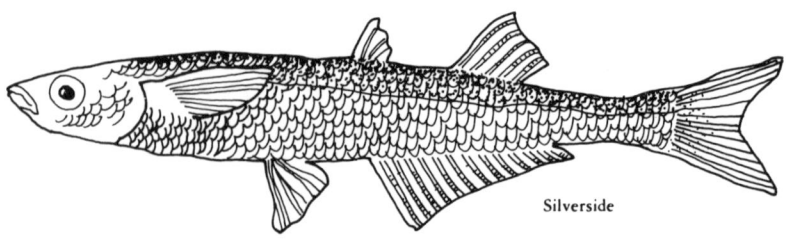

Silverside

Seine Nets

A seine net is a net about three or four feet high and from ten to fifty feet long. It has floats on the top and lead weights on the bottom. The ends of the net are tied to poles about six feet long. The size of the mesh can vary, but quarter or half-inch mesh is best.

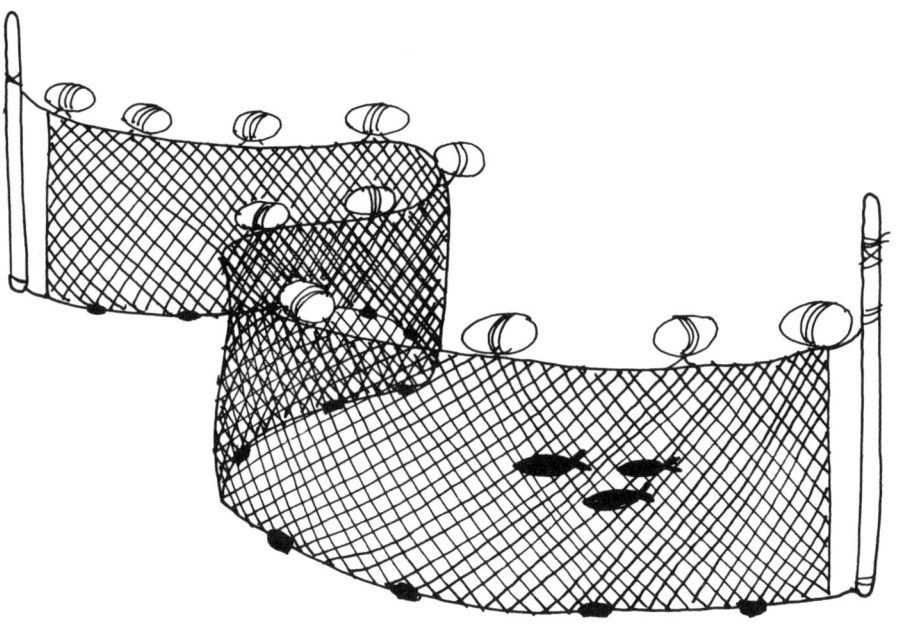

When seining, you need a partner — one person for each end of the net — though I will describe some single person operations later. Choose a stretch of water that has the right depth. The mouth of the net should reach from the surface to the bottom, and the bottom should be smooth enough so you can walk and so the net won't snag. One person takes the deep end and strikes straight out from shore while the other person stays in knee-depth water. When the net is fully extended, you are ready to pull the net through a stretch of water.

To do this, turn and face in the opposite direction to the way you plan to walk; then start walking backward. Keep the bottom of the pole on the bay bottom. It's easiest, I think, to pull with one hand near the top of the pole and the other about eighteen inches below the top hand, but try different styles until you're comfortable. The person on the deep end should be about five to ten feet ahead of you, but both of you are pulling the net along bottom as you walk backwards.

I usually cover about twenty-five to fifty yards of water and then start the pull-in. To do this, the person near the shore slows or stops his pull, while the person on the deep end swings toward shore in a semi-circle until he is in shallow water. Then, both of you draw the net up on shore, making sure that the weights stay right on the bottom.

Once the net is up out of the water, you should fold it over on itself so that the catch is in the pocket of the net with mesh above and below it. This keeps the bait in the net and keeps it damp. Then, go through the net, sorting out what you want to keep.

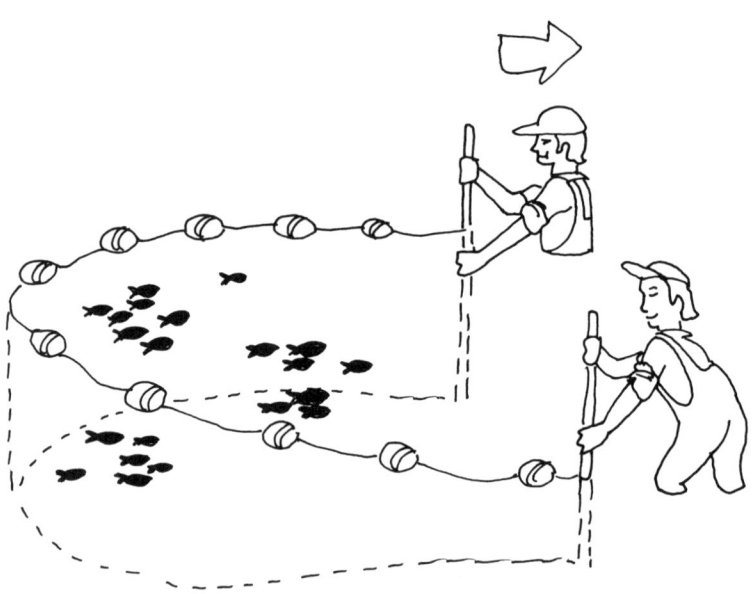

Be sure to let everything that you don't want go back into the water. You can do this by picking out what you want and then walking the net back into a foot of water and dumping it, or by picking out what you don't want and tossing it back. In any case, don't leave your excess catch out on the dry beach to die and rot; it should be put back where it came from.

When you are through seining for the day, wash the net and pick out all the seaweed. Seaweed left in a net can cause it to rot quickly. Then, back at the house, rinse the net in fresh water and hang it out to dry.

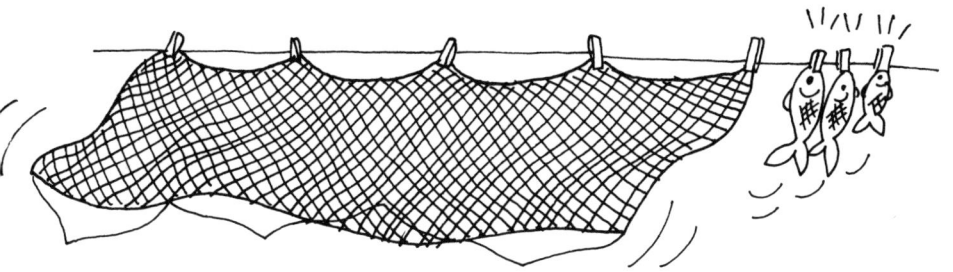

A good cotton seine will last a dozen years if it is well cared for. I have found that braided nylon seines are even better. They are lighter, easier to clean, and they seem to last forever. But don't hang a synthetic material net in the sun or it will weaken. And when a seine gets a hole in it, patch it soon. Once it starts to get too many holes, you'll begin to lose too much of your catch and you will be inclined to throw away a net that would have given you another decade of service if you had kept up with the mending.

Here are two ways to use a seine by yourself if you cannot find a helper. First, make a second, smaller seine, called a simple seine, about four feet long and with a pole at each end. Walk through the shallows with the seine in front of you, holding a pole in each hand. Keep the weights on the bottom and hold the poles at an angle so they touch the bottom about a foot or so in front of you.

In a pinch, you can tie one end of the seine down to the shore, or drive one pole into the bottom just off shore, and pull the other end in a circle around the fixed end. Neither of these methods will do as good a job, but I've caught enough bait this way more than once.

Two other points about seining — often I go to the beach with a seine and ask a passerby to do the shallow end for me. Many people, especially the kids, are delighted to be asked, and they get interested if you take a little time to explain what you are doing. Also, seining is simply fun by itself, regardless of its practicality. It is a superb way to learn what kind of bait (forage) fish are around, and you also learn about the juvenile forms of larger fish. For example, I have found specimens of small kingfish, spot, croaker, mullet, snapper bluefish, winter flounder, weakfish, tiny striped bass, several kinds of killifish, pipefish, seahorse, tautog, cunner, mackerel, stickleback, pollock, haddock, sea robins, and puffers. In fact, seining for fish is a great way to stock a saltwater aquarium. But again — **be sure to put back alive what you don't need or want.**

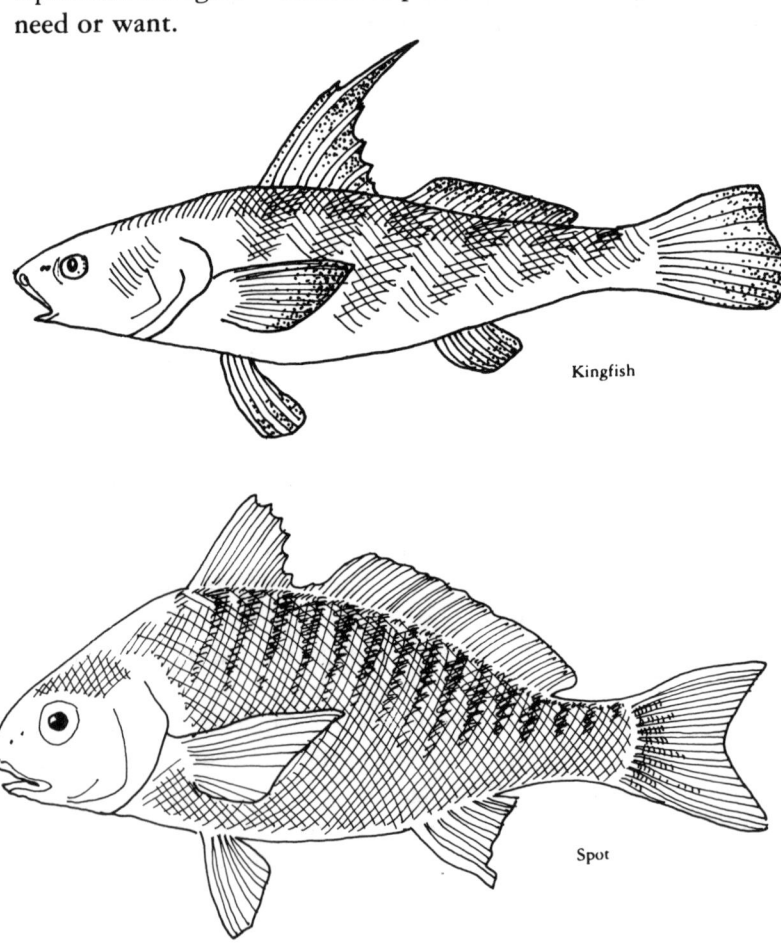

Kingfish

Spot

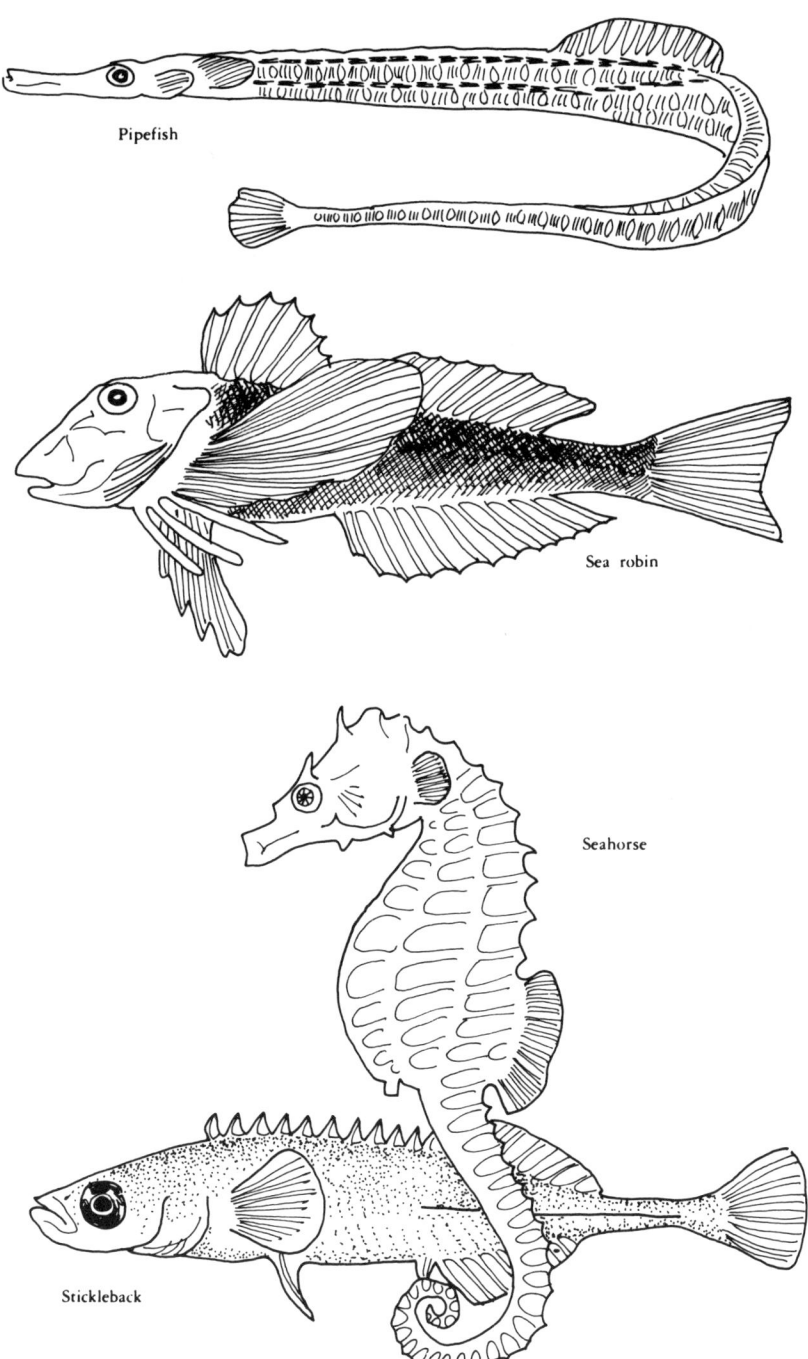

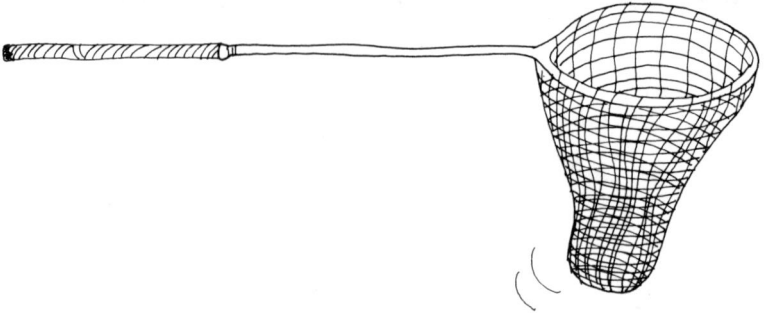

Dip Nets

Dip nets can also be used to catch bait. Mine has small, one-eighth inch mesh. It has a ring twenty inches across, a pocket about two feet deep, and is mounted on a stout seven-foot handle. With such a net, you can scoop bait without help. Its disadvantage is that you can cover only a small amount of water with each scoop.

Dip nets are especially handy for covering pilings, bulkheads, and edges where shallow water drops off to deep. One good way to use such a net is to extend it in front of you and then draw it in to your feet, but the usual way is to walk with it in shallow water, say up to your knees or a little deeper. Hold the net in front of you, its loop front rubbing right on the bottom. Walk fairly quickly and check the net every ten paces.

Sometimes it makes sense to turn and cover the area you have just done, as small minnows will come into that spot, feeding on little bits of food you have stirred up. I have had good luck catching killies, silversides, and shrimp with such a net.

It's best to use a dip net in and on the edges of grass beds and along stream edges. Smooth bay bottoms are usually unproductive.

One good trick with a dip net is to re-form the front of the net so it is straight across. That way, when you are scooping, the whole front edge of the net is on the bottom. Again, wash your net after use.

Cast Nets

Cast nets (also called throw nets) are good bait catchers and are fun to use. They work like this: the net is in the form of a circle, about eight feet in diameter when spread out. The bottom of the net is weighed, and a set of strings runs from the net edge up through an opening at the top of the net. These strings pass through a ring at the top of the net and are connected to a line about fifteen to twenty-five feet long. The other end of the line has a loop in it and is tied to your wrist.

There are too many variations of net throwing techniques to describe here — holding a part of the net in your teeth (probably only used in the movies), draping a part of the net over your arm, or whatever — but the principle is the same for all methods.

What you do is throw the net out so that it hits the surface of the water fully spread, in as perfect a circle as you can achieve. Then the weights carry the net down. Usually, you are netting in shallow water and you let the weights take the net to the bottom. Then, as you pull back on the line, the net closes (purses), and the bait is trapped inside. Once it's closed, you pull the net ashore and empty it.

My cast net is twenty-five years old, and was made of cotton twine in North Carolina. The ring is made of brass, but some of the real "pro" nets from that area have a hollow piece of cow horn for the ring. I have patched the net yearly and have replaced the draw strings at least five times. It still catches fish.

Here is how I throw it (I'm right handed): loosely coil the line in your right hand, gathering coils between thumb and forefinger. Then, reach down with the left hand and grasp a bit of the net's bottom edge, bring it up, and grab it with that busy right thumb and forefinger. Reach down again and take another part of the net's bottom edge with your left thumb and forefinger, about two feet away from where you picked up the first part of the edge. Now, if you hold both hands in front of you at chest height, you should have the net out front and somewhat open.

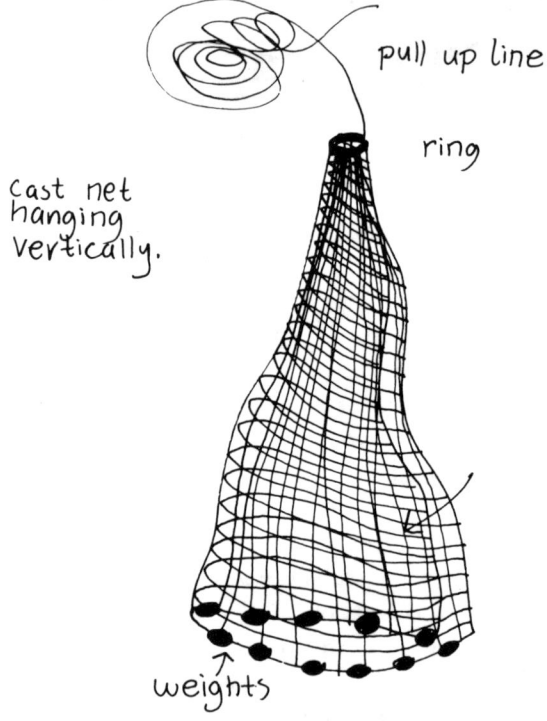

You are now ready to throw. Move the left foot forward and swing your shoulders and arms to the right — this is the back part of the throw. Then, move your arms, shoulders, and body to the left, making sure the bottom of the net doesn't drag. When the net is in front of you, let go with the right hand and, a split second later, with the left hand — sort of like throwing a giant discus. The net should fly out in front of you about five or ten feet, hit the water in a circle and drop to the bottom, ready for pursing.

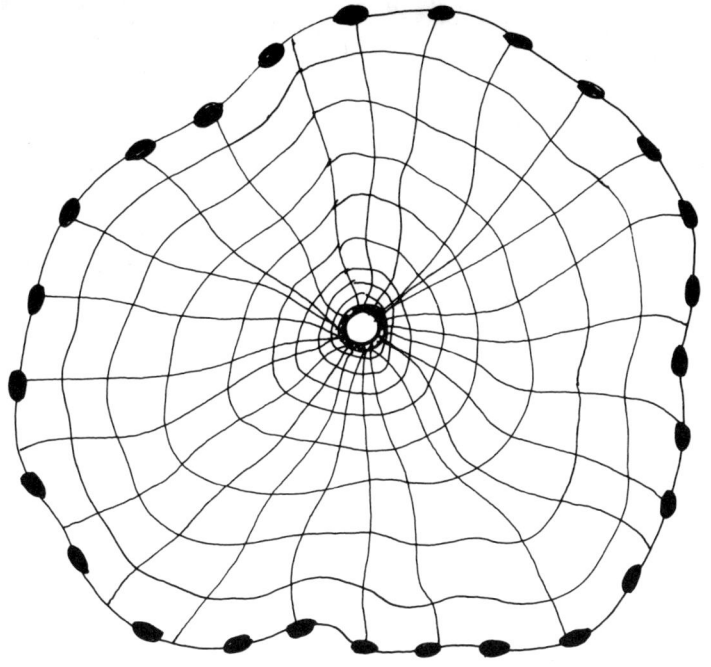

..... as the fish see net descending to them.

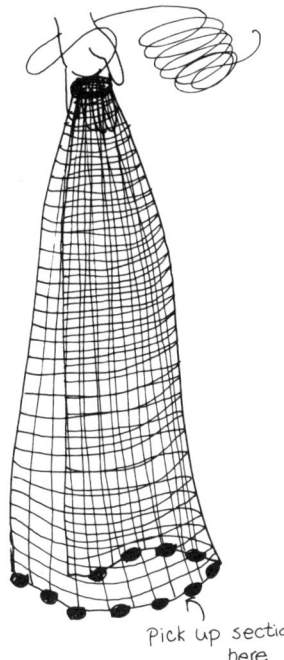

This describes what I would call a forehand throw. Many people cast backhand, but the principle is the same. Your best bet is either to watch someone else do it and copy, or to get your own net and practice, preferably on a lonely beach if you are easily embarrassed. Stick with it — it sounds harder than it is. With practice, you'll be able to cast with the best of them.

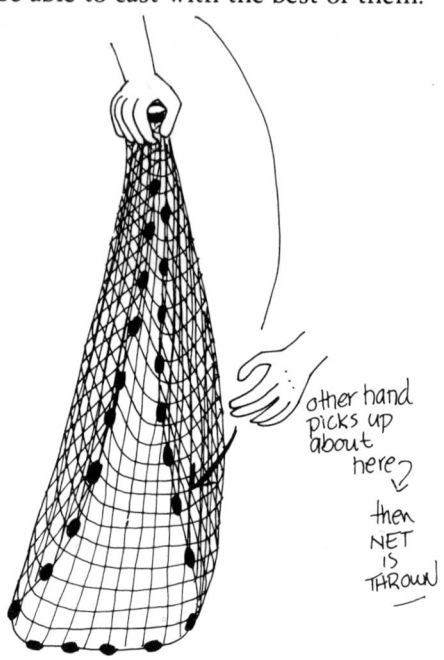

Learning when to cast — learning where fish are — is tougher. Most seining is "blind-netting"; you pull through an area and see what there is, if anything. With cast-netting, you must find some baitfish, figure out what kind they are, which way they are heading and how fast they're swimming. Here are a few tips, mostly for **mullet**, prime prey of cast netters.   Mullet, superb

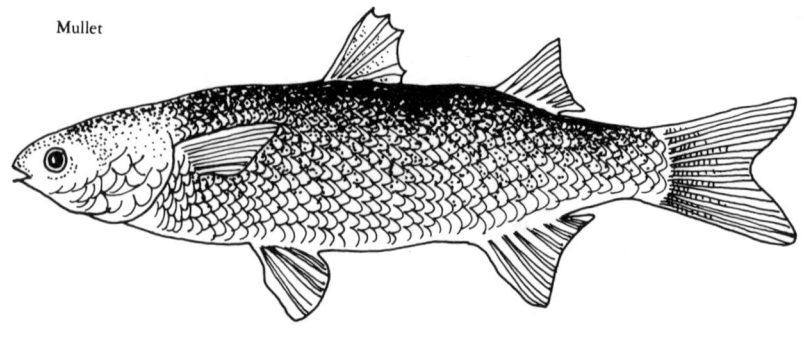

Mullet

baitfish, live in brackish creeks in the northeast during the summer. They are particularly common from Cape Cod south. In late summer as nights cool, mullet leave their creeks, start moving into bays and inlets, and then go out through the inlets and south along the beaches, heading for the Carolinas and points south. These are usually small fish, up to five inches in length.

When cast-netting, you should see the prey before you cast. Blind-casting with a cast net is good exercise, but it catches little. A mullet school makes a special kind of fluttering motion on the surface of the water, almost like a little puff of wind. As you spend more and more time looking for them, you will learn to recognize the special flutter that a mullet school makes, so that you will even be able to spot a school in fairly rough water. Just look for an irregular pattern to the water's surface. Also, mullet almost always stay close to shore when undisturbed — they are usually within wading distance.

Mullet are extremely edgy, and they appear to have good eyesight. So when you see a school, avoid lots of movement, and don't tread heavily on the sand, mud, or shore. I prefer to get down low and walk very gently.

Figure out which way the school is traveling and get far enough ahead of it so you can hunker down and wait for it to get within casting range. Then leap to the task. Get up to full height and cast quickly. Try to hit the front of the school right on the kisser. Let the net drop and try to cast only in water shallow enough for the net to get to the bottom fast, say three or four feet deep.

In the surf, mullet will also show the telltale fluttering on the surface. At other times, you can see the school in a wave just before it breaks. And often, the mullet will tumble in, or be chased in by big fish so they are right in the wave's wash. This is an excellent time to throw the net, when the school is confused.

Casting a net is fun. It is almost like fishing itself. Try carrying a cast net when you walk a beach or bay. There are times when you will see a school of fish. A cast of the net will help you identify them. Then, if you have no use for the catch, let it go.

Traps

Traps are net or wire containers designed with openings that small fish can enter easily but exit with difficulty. The basic trap for minnows is a cylinder with funnel openings at each end. The cylinder opens in the middle for baiting and for emptying the catch. Good bait for traps includes crushed clam or mussels, cut fish, fish heads or racks (backbones after filleting), or bread.

Put the trap in any tidal stream so that it will be underwater even at low tide. Tie a rope to it and tie the end to a stick anchored in the mud or stream bank, or to a buoy. Most of the time you can pop a trap in the water, wait for an hour, and have bait.

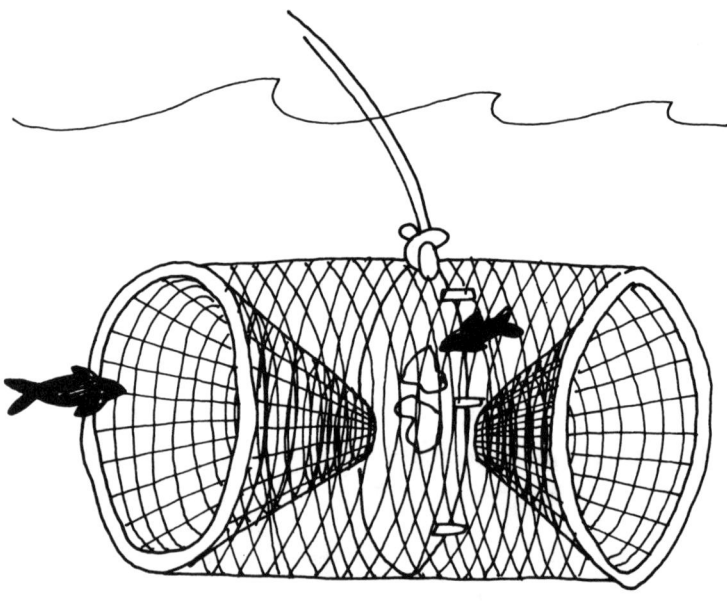

You can also catch bait with a dip trap which you can make. Get a square of metal mosquito netting about three feet on a side. Use aluminum; steel will rust in a week. Tie some line to each corner and make a bridle, then tie a line to the bridle. Put some weights (a rock) in the middle, wire down some bait, and drop the dip trap in a likely spot. Wait three minutes and pull it up and you'll have some bait.

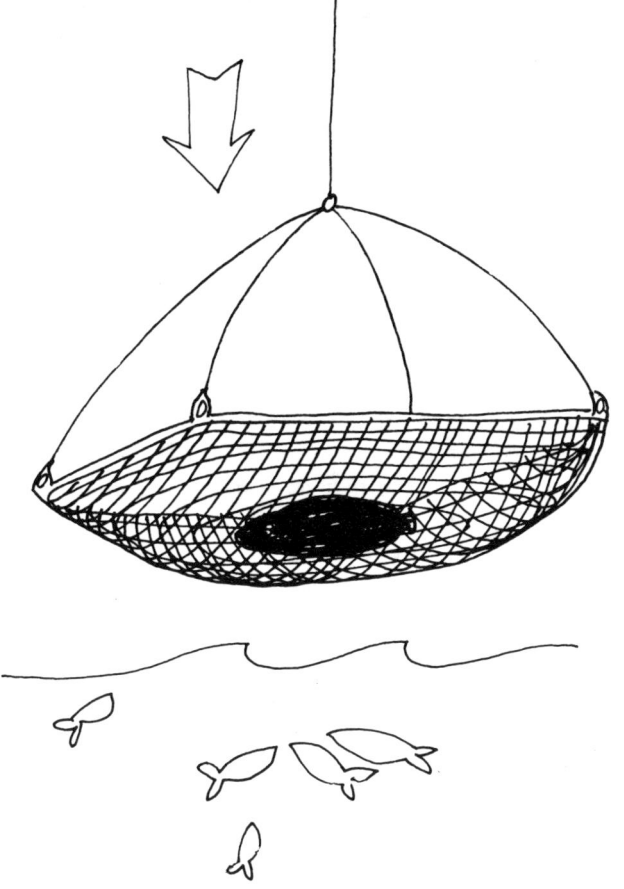

Here's a special trick for catching killies. Put a piece of soft bait — mussel or clam belly, the softer the better — on a hook or a hairpin that's been bent out and up to form a small hook. Tie the pin or hook to light line and a pole and drop it where killies hang out. Let a couple of killies start to swallow the bait, then pull them up fast and hold them over a bucket. They'll drop off. Put the hook back in and catch some more. Sometimes this will get you killies when all else fails, and if you are taking a small child out fishing, the killie fishing itself is an afternoon of fun.

Now, here is a rundown of some of the baitfish you can catch with the equipment above.

Killies

Killies (mummichogs, minnows, "minnas" — they go by any number of names) can be caught by any of the methods above. They can be caught in rivers, bays, swamps, and streams, from early spring to late fall, and are usually found in water with a hard mud bottom. They are the best bait for fluke (summer flounder).

Killies are also one of the easiest of the baitfish to keep alive and well. A killie box is best for boat-fishing. It is a box with a wire bottom that lets water circulate through it. Just hang it over the side of the boat, but be sure to pull the box out of the water when you are motoring from one fishing spot to another. Drop it back in when you stop to fish, and the killies will be fine all day.

You can also keep killies in wet seaweed, newspaper, or cloth. The secret is not to let the killies get warm. Keep them in the shade and dip the weed or other material in the water once in a while. You can keep killies in a refrigerator overnight in wet weed. In fact, they keep better in weed than they do in a bucket of water.

If you insist on keeping them in a bucket, replace the water frequently. Killies will use up the oxygen in a bucket of water in an hour or so, especially on a warm day, then they will suffocate. In damp cool weed, their gills will be damp and they can pull oxygen out of the air as long as their gills don't dry out.

Killies are about the only baitfish that you can keep alive easily for long periods of time. A few others can be kept with air pumps, and are good bait. Among them:

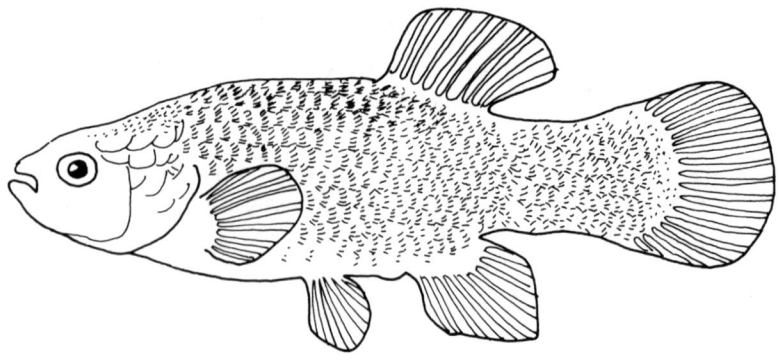

Bunker

Bunker (moss bunker, pogies, menhaden) — these fish get to about a pound, though you will be able to net smaller ones. They are super bait for striped bass, weakfish, and bluefish when fished live. Hook them gently through the back and allow them to swim freely on an unweighted line.

Often you will come across a school of bunker in a bay, in a river, or along the beach, the bunker flashing and swirling at or near the surface. One way to catch and fish them live is to cast into the school with a bare treble hook, casting the hook across the school's path and reeling and jerking it through the school until you snag one. Then you can just let the fish swim off with your hook in its back. That wounded, slightly differently swimming bunker will often attract a big fish very quickly.

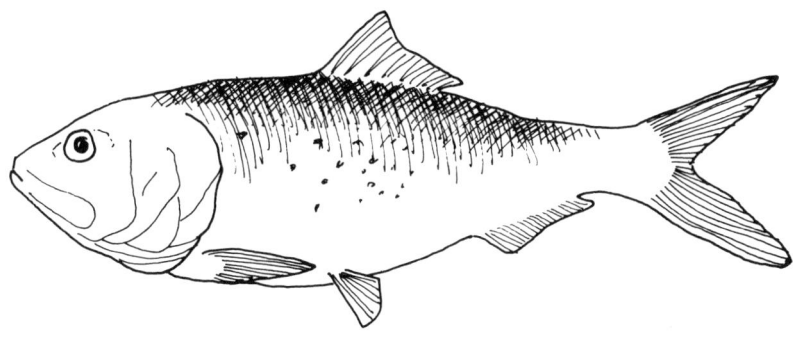

Mullet

Mullet were covered previously. It is possible to fish them live by hooking one gently through the back, casting it out, and letting it swim. Mullet die quickly this way, but they catch fish. Mullet can be kept alive in a bucket for half an hour if you keep just a few. Have a top on the bucket — mullet are great jumpers.

Mullet, bunker, and mackerel are good bait for bluefish if cut in strips or chunks, and whole, dead mullet can be fished with a special hook. This rig has a piece of strong stainless steel wire with a loop in the end, and comes with a double hook. Stick the wire down the mullet's throat and out the vent (anus). Then place the hook through the loop and hook it into the side of the mullet, or simply pull the wire up into the fish until the two hooks are at the vent. This rig is good for stripers, weakfish, and bluefish.

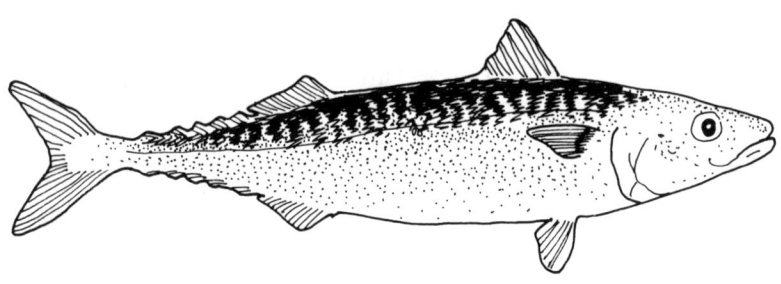

The remaining fish listed can be used dead, either whole or in strips or chunks.

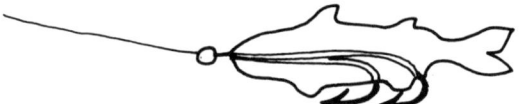

Silversides and Anchovies

Silversides (shiners) and anchovies are two kinds of small, thin, silvery fish that often clog a seine. They are used whole and are good bait for bluefish, especially small snapper (six to twelve inches in length).I have caught fluke on large silversides. Smelt are good fluke bait and large silversides are like small smelt.

Eels

Eels are a special bait for striped bass. They are fished whole and dead, or as dressed and rigged skins. They are good for striped bass at night, especially when fished near jetties.

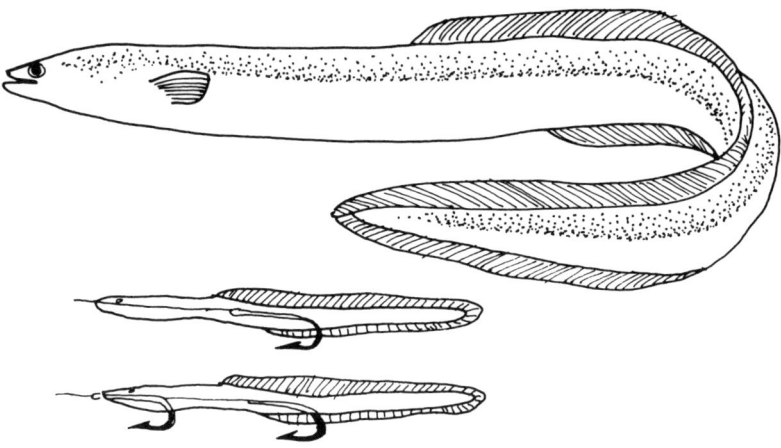

Chunks or strips of other fish are often good bait, and sometimes the best. Strips cut from fluke or sea robin are good fluke bait. Live spot (lafayette) are good for blues and weakfish, and chunks of butterfish can be used as bait.

In fact, any fish that you catch can be considered bait.

6. CHUMMING

Earlier under "Mussels" I mentioned chumming, a way of attracting fish. Almost all of the bait covered in this book can be used as chum, though the most common chum bait is either crushed shellfish — clam, mussels, or hard crabs — or chopped fish, usually bunker or mullet, though any fish scraps will do.

This chum is put in a chum pot and used while boat fishing. You can make your own pot out of hardware cloth. I simply take a section of it two feet square, fold it over and wire the bottom and sides together. Then I toss the chum and a brick inside, pinch or

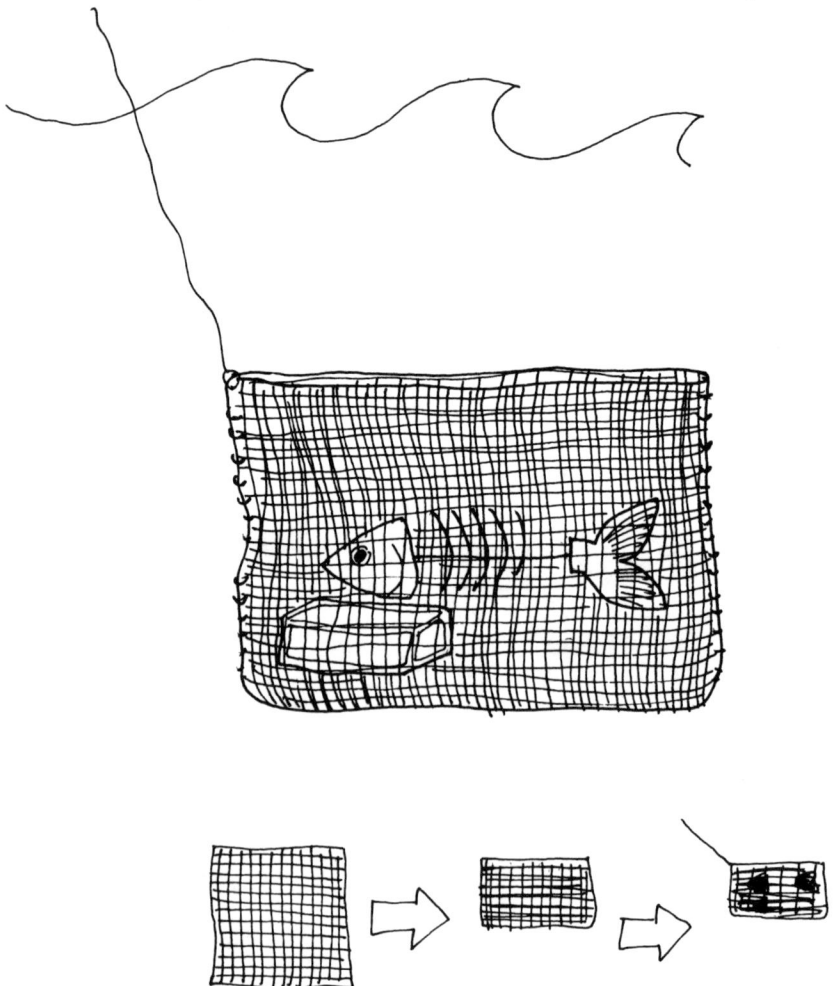

wire the top shut, and lower the whole thing down to the bottom on a line. Then I fish on the side of the boat that puts me "downstream" in the tidal current. The little bits of clam or fish wash out of the pot and swirl down the tidal current attracting fish. It's a good rig for bottom fish, especially winter flounder and kingfish.

You can also chum for bluefish with chopped bunker or mullet — the finer the chop, the better. One method is to run a dozen bunker through a meat grinder, mix the meat with a cup of water, and keep it cool until ready for use. Then ladle this "soup" over the side of the boat; the "slick" formed is a proven bluefish attractor.

Small bluefish — snappers — can sometimes be chummed with chopped silversides. Cut a bunch up into pieces and dribble them into the water.

In closing, here is a list of tips on bait that you can catch yourself:

-- Fresh bait is always best. If you don't plan to use your bait right away, get it on ice as soon as possible. You can freeze it, but remember: freezing bait softens it, so be prepared either to tie frozen bait on with a thread, or salt it, as adding salt toughens bait.

-- Be sure that, when you are digging shellfish or worms for bait, you obey the local laws. Many areas are closed to shellfishing because of pollution, and some mud flats are private property.

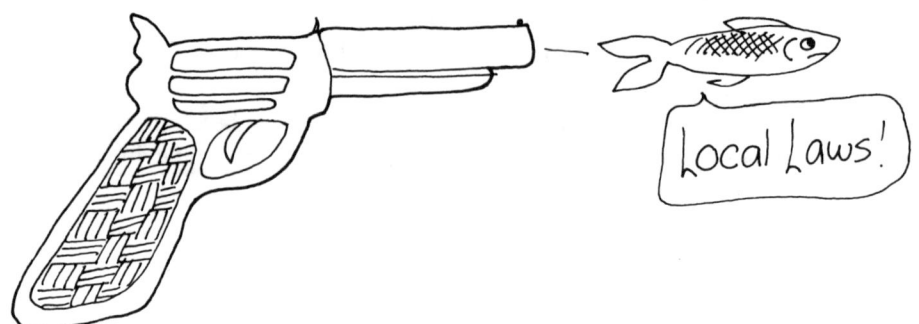

-- Some baits that you catch or dig in salt water are good freshwater bait. Try killies as a live bait for freshwater bass, and saltwater shrimp are great bait for many freshwater species. Killies are especially good for ice fishing if you can't get other live bait.

-- Again, don't catch, kill, and keep more bait than you need. Keep what you are going to use that day, the next day, or for freezing, and let the rest go.

-- And finally, remember that getting your own bait can be fun and it can help you understand how the lives of different marine animals are intertwined. But, if you want to get off by yourself and fish for an hour, and that's all the time you have, then drop into your local bait store. Buy a few worms or a piece of squid and go out and have fun.

In closing, let's say you took your seine out and caught fifty fair-sized silversides. You went over to the dock, tried for snapper blues for an hour, used ten of the silversides for bait, caught nothing, and now you're headed for home. Don't despair! Dinner is right there in your bucket. Take those silversides, cut off the heads, and squeeze out the innards between your thumb and forefinger. Rinse them well, roll them lightly in cracker crumbs, and fry them for four minutes in a hot pan of butter. One man's bait is another man's supper!

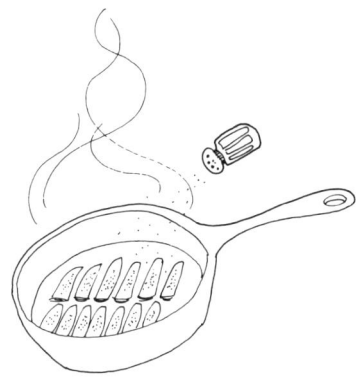

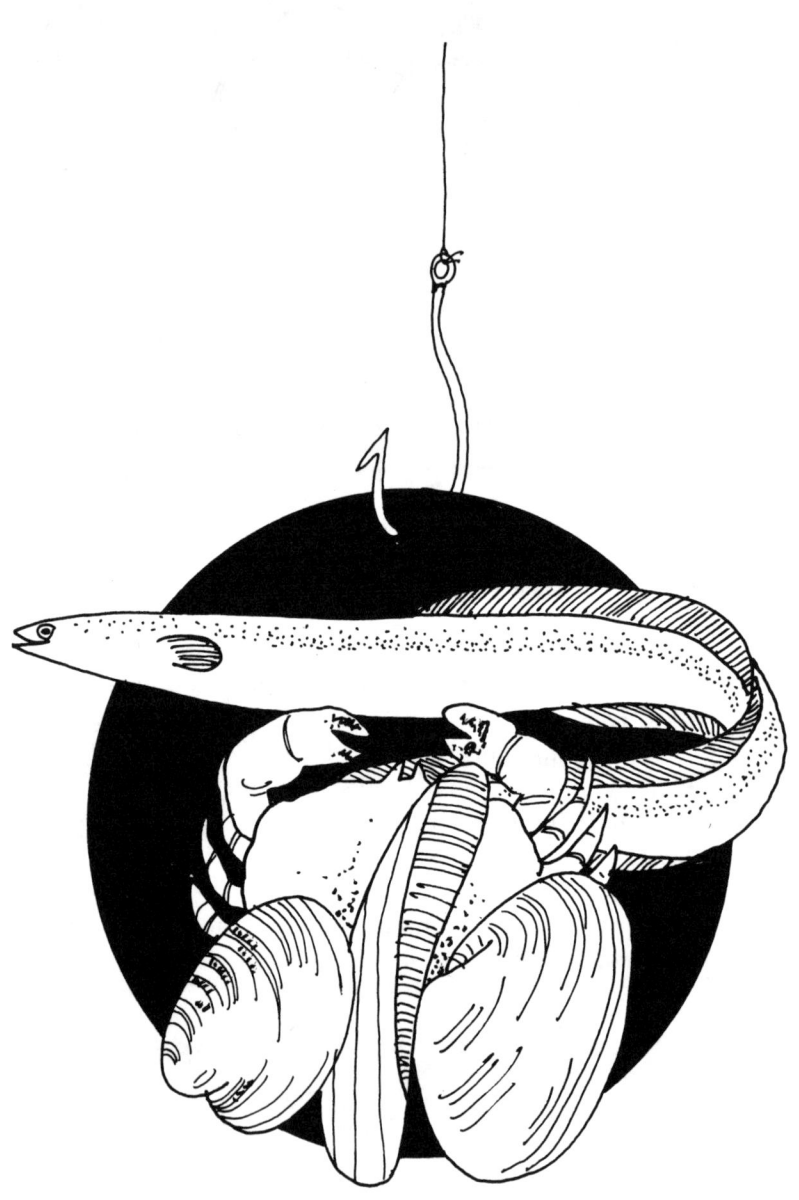

Notes

Record bait species caught, date, time of day, weather, location, how caught (how detected), degree of success.
GOOD RECORDS MAKE GOOD CATCHES.

Notes

Notes

Notes

Notes

Notes

Notes

Notes

Notes

Notes